ENTERTAINING WITH

Betsy
Bloomingdale

ENTERTAINING WITH

Betsy

Bloomingdale

A Collection of Culinary Tips and Treasures from the
World's Best Hosts and Hostesses

WITH CATHERINE WHITNEY

The recipe for Lobster Mousseline on page 90 is from *The White House Family Cookbook* by Henry Haller & Virginia Aronson. Copyright © 1987 by Henry Haller & Virginia Aronson. Reprinted by permission of Random House, Inc.

Beautiful America Publishing Company ©

P.O. Box 646

Wilsonville, Oregon 97070

Design: Jacelen Pete

Editing: Andrea Tronslin

Editorial Research: Sharon Maasdam: Home Economist for *The Oregonian*

Linotronic Output: LeFont Laser Imaging and Design

Printed in Korea

SAMHWA PRINTING COMPANY, LTD.

Library of Congress Cataloging-in-Publication Data

Bloomingdale, Betsy.

Entertaining with Betsy Bloomingdale : a collection of culinary tips and treasures from the world's best hosts and hostesses / with Catherine Whitney.

p. cm. Includes Index.

ISBN 0-89802-633-4 $29.95

1. Entertaining. 2. Menus. 3. Cookery. I. Whitney, Catherine (Catherine A.) II. Title.

TX731.B574 1994

642 .4--dc20

93-38988

CIP

To my children:

Geoffrey, Lisa, and Robert

Acknowledgments

Writing this book has been such a wonderful experience, thanks to all the support I've received. I am most grateful to Ted Paul and his fine staff at Beautiful America Publishing, who have given me encouragement every step of the way; and to my collaborator, Catherine Whitney, who has helped me organize all of my material into book form.

I am most appreciative of my friends who have been so generous with their time and effort on my behalf. They've all gone out of their way to share their favorite recipes, menus, and entertaining tips. This book could never have happened without their contribution. In a sense, this is their book too, and I hope they feel as proud of it as I do.

Author's Note

I have had the pleasure of making or tasting many of the recipes. In fact, I've begged for some of them for this book. Others are favorites of friends who have kindly shared. I look forward to trying them, as I hope you will.

CONTENTS

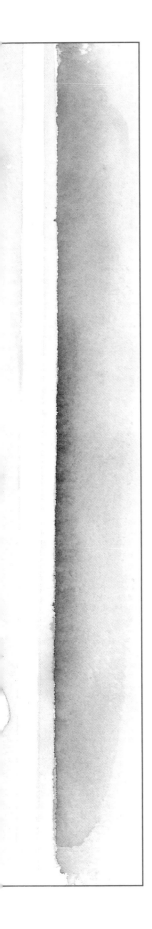

CHAPTER ONE

The Joy of Entertaining

HOW I GREW TO LOVE IT

I have wanted to write this book for a long time—to bring together all of my personal experiences, the ideas of my many imaginative friends, and the simple advice that has been passed down to me through the years. Entertaining is not a frivolous endeavor. I believe it is one of the great essentials of life. These are among our basic human needs: To bring pleasure to others, to share one's home and table, to give of oneself. Food, beautifully prepared, can be an inspiration. If you doubt that, just think of all the significant things that happen around a dinner table or at a party. How many important decisions are made over meals? How many marriages are born at parties? How many lifetime friends are found in the midst of a lively conversation that takes place in someone else's house?

When I talk about entertaining, I am not just talking about menus, guest lists, flowers, and table settings. I am talking about the activity that brings us together on a human level to share our houses and open our hearts to the people we admire and care for. That's the essence.

Of course, it took me time to learn this. As a child, I viewed learning to cook and be a hostess as something one did as a matter of course. For my generation of women, it was part of our basic education.

When I was growing up, our kitchen was the center of the household. My mother was a natural cook, and she took it seriously. She encouraged me to learn from her, and I was always looking over her shoulder. When my parents entertained, I would put on my party dress and pass the appetizers or help in some other way. My mother thought it was important for me to feel comfortable in social situations with grown-ups.

Later, as a teenager, I began to entertain myself, and my mother also encouraged this. I would organize parties or lunches for my girlfriends, and I learned to love being a hostess. I found it so much fun to make people happy in this way.

My mother loved to repeat the old adage that the way to a man's heart was through his stomach. She firmly believed that every young woman should attend cooking school before marriage, so off I went one summer vacation to the Hillcliff School of Cookery. There I learned to make the special dishes designed to dazzle a man.

By the time I started going out with Alfred Bloomingdale, I could make a few special things. My favorite, and the one of which I was most proud, was a lemon soufflé. If there was such a thing as a dish to sweep a man off his feet, this was it!

Sure enough, Alfred raved about the soufflé, and in my naiveté, I served it to him over and over again. It wasn't until after we were married that he said to me, "I loathe lemon desserts. Never make that soufflé again!" He'd only been pretending, in order to please me. Needless to say, lemon soufflé was taken off the menu. This was a good lesson for me. I learned that what one serves is important, but the spirit with which it is served is even more important. Alfred said, "I never dared tell you how I felt about that soufflé, because you presented it every time like a gift from heaven."

After I was married, I continued to study and improve my cooking. It had become a great pleasure for me. At one point while we were staying in New York City, I took a class from Dione Lucas, a famous private cooking teacher who held classes in the historic Dakota, that wonderful gothic building that has become home to so many noted people. Alfred and I were staying at an Eastside hotel. He conducted his business, and I went off to Dione Lucas's and learned to prepare elaborate dishes that I could serve at parties. I still remember one occasion, coming out of the Dakota on a cold day and hopping into a cab, holding a large Chartreuse mousse dessert I had just prepared. As I stepped from the cab in front of the hotel, I slipped on the icy sidewalk and the dessert plopped to the ground, splattering in a puddle at the feet of the doorman. It was my first calamity, and I was distraught. But Alfred thought it was the funniest thing he'd ever heard. He taught me to laugh through calamity.

"My mother loved to repeat the old adage that the way to a man's heart was through his stomach."

For him, every disaster could be turned around. He had a remarkable tolerance for human error, and I suppose it's what made him such a good businessman. I recall one time Alfred and I were invited someplace for dinner, and when we arrived our friends were beside themselves. There had been a fight with the couple who cooked for them and the cooks had walked out leaving dinner unprepared. "Never mind," said Alfred cheerfully. "I'll get dinner." He jumped in the car and drove off, only to return fifteen minutes later with an enormous bucket of Kentucky Fried Chicken. Of course, we had a marvelous time.

I began to realize that beneath my love of cooking and my desire to master the art was a genuine delight in giving pleasure to my friends. It put everything into perspective, and I grew less nervous about being a hostess.

One of the best things I ever did for my family and my kitchen was to hire a Chinese cook named Lau. He taught me more about cooking than anyone else. Lau was a delight. Everyone in the house loved to go into the kitchen and see his serene, happy face. He made cooking fun, and he would try almost anything. He loved to experiment, and he was anxious to learn new ideas. Since Lau couldn't read English, I began to get more and more involved in the kitchen. I would read the recipes to him and we would make them together. Sometimes I would show him a picture in a magazine and he would smile and nod and make it from sight. Other times, I would bring him ideas from restaurants. On one occasion, I slipped a couple of vegetables carved like flowers into my purse so Lau could duplicate them for a dinner I was planning.

It was such a joy to spend days in the kitchen with Lau and his sunny disposition. He was a born cook who worked by instinct—a pinch here, a dab there. He never tested the oven, but could tell the temperature by sticking in his hand. Back home in Shanghai, Lau had cooked on a wood-burning stove, and he learned to make his own judgments without the help of modern appliances. He was a true artist, and he also taught my children how to cook.

Alfred and I loved to entertain, and when the children were young, our favorite parties were small, noisy affairs where we'd invite our friends and their children. On other occasions, we would entertain more formally. When Alfred started Diner's Club, our guests would often include people from all over the

"Alfred taught me to laugh through calamity. For him, every disaster could be turned around."

world. It was a challenge, but I never once saw Lau get ruffled. It didn't matter if we were expecting six or sixty guests; it was all the same to him.

Lau was with us for many years. He finally retired at the age of eighty-two, after Alfred passed away. He's still alive today, now well into his nineties. His recipes have become staples of my family cookbook, and whenever I serve one of Lau's dishes, I can almost feel his presence in the room.

From the Sublime to the Homey

While my favorite style of entertaining remains casual and family oriented, I have to admit I've thoroughly enjoyed being exposed to some of the best parties in the world. When I give my lectures, the women love to hear the stories—especially those involving European royalty. Although we Americans love our democracy and wouldn't have it any other way, we are fascinated with the details of how royalty lives in other parts of the world. It reminds us of fairy tales and I must say, there have been times when I've found it easy to imagine I was in a fairy tale.

One scene that stands out is the Easter I spent in Germany with Prince and Princess von Thurn und Taxis—Johannes and Gloria. Johannes has since died, and Gloria is now the subject of great interest because she has been left with one of the biggest fortunes in Europe.

I accepted their invitation to spend Easter a few years ago at Saint Emmeran, their castle in Regensburg. It was quite memorable. Saint Emmeran had, if you can imagine this, five hundred fully furnished rooms—and it was only one of eleven castles they owned! My room and sitting room were done in red brocade. The bed was the most intimidating high-standing affair I'd ever seen—like something right out of "The Princess and the Pea"—and I worried that I wouldn't be able to figure out how to get into it.

One detail I especially remember is that there were clocks everywhere. There were four in my room alone, and each morning at 11 o'clock, a man dressed in full Alpine livery would arrive to wind them.

Dining with Gloria and Johannes was quite special. There was a footman behind every chair, something you just don't see these days. I know it was new for me.

Princess Margaret was also a guest that weekend. When she entered the magnificent castle, she gasped and exclaimed, "Oh my, this place is bigger than Buckingham!"

Gloria has given me a recipe that appears later in the book. Perhaps when you prepare it, you can imagine sitting at their long table with its pristine white damask tablecloth and shining silver.

It may be true that Buckingham Palace can't measure up to the German castles of Thurn und Taxis, but I certainly never noticed it. Buckingham Palace is magnificent. When I attended the royal wedding of Prince Charles and Lady Diana Spencer, I had the persistent feeling that I was taking a walk through history. Later, I visited Earl and Countess Spencer (now Countess Cambrun), Princess Diana's father and stepmother, at their castle, Althrop, which is two hours from London. Happily, a tour of the house was on the agenda, and with all the famous paintings on the walls, it felt like a museum. But the Spencers were hardly formal themselves. We had become friends, and I enjoyed their warmth and humor. Countess Spencer's old family recipe for traditional steak and kidney pie appears later in the book.

Even royalty can be down to earth—which is certainly true of the British royal family. On the 200th anniversary of America's independence I traveled to London to spend the occasion at Winfield House with Carol and Charles Price, our ambassador to the Court of St. James at the time. One evening they took me to dinner at the home of David Frost, and the guests included the young Prince Andrew and Sarah Ferguson. This was before they married. They were so relaxed and so much fun. At one point, I walked into the garden holding an hors d'oeuvre in a napkin in my hand. I was standing talking to Prince Andrew and wondering what to do with it since I had no plans to eat it. "I don't know why I took this," I said finally.

He laughed. "Just toss it."

"Toss it? What do you mean?"

He motioned toward the garden. "Just toss it right there in the bushes. I won't tell."

So I did.

Prince Charles is quieter than his brother, but he's very sincere and he has a good sense of irony. Once during the Reagan years, he was visiting the United States, and we were at a reception together in Florida. The Prince pulled me aside.

"Mrs. Bloomingdale," he said, "I've been trying to reach Mrs. Reagan at the White House and I can't get through."

"I'll give you the number," I offered.

He shook his head helplessly. "I have the number. It's just that when I call and say, 'This is the Prince of Wales and I'd like to speak to Mrs. Reagan,' the operator says, 'Yes, sir, but who is this really?'"

I had to laugh. What a dilemma! I made the call for him and he got through.

> *"On many occasions, I've reciprocated for the marvelous times I've had abroad. Of course, as I've learned, when you entertain people, you must remember from whence they come."*

On many occasions, I've reciprocated for the marvelous times I've had abroad. Of course, as I've learned, when you entertain people you must remember from whence they come. A friend of mine, a prominent Saudi Arabian woman, visited me not long ago in California and I decided to take her and her husband to dinner at Morton's, which is a favorite restaurant of mine. I arrived early so I could make arrangements for the restaurant to send me the bill. As a woman alone, I don't like to sign the check in front of my guests.

When my friends arrived, they immediately called the waiter over and ordered red wine. I nearly fainted when I saw what they'd chosen—a Château Lafite-Rothschild that cost over $300 a bottle. Later, when they ordered a second bottle, I smiled bravely, but you can imagine what was going through my head.

Of course, my friends assumed they were paying for dinner and when they discovered I had already taken care of the check, they were dreadfully embarrassed. But I took it in stride. "I wanted you to be happy," I said. "And if that made you happy, it's fine with me." Alfred would have laughed.

The Secret to Entertaining

The real secret of entertaining, when you strip away all the layers of lavishness, wealth, and spectacle, is: You can have all the money and privilege in the world and possess no style. You can spend a fortune on the most elaborate parties and leave your guests feeling bored and let down. Real style comes from within.

Much has been made of the fabulous entertaining styles of the rich and famous. But all of this means nothing if one does not possess the inner qualities.

I believe every woman, regardless of her circumstances, can be a wonderful hostess if she possesses and expresses the following:

1. Warmth
2. Attention to detail
3. Creativity
4. Genuine caring
5. Joy in life

For me, there is no greater pleasure than to invite people to my house. Entertaining is the way I express my love and friendship. I have always believed there is no great trick to being a successful hostess. Simply put, a perfect hostess is a person who makes her guests happy to be present—whether she's giving a formal dinner or a cup of tea. She seems to accomplish this effortlessly, but behind the scenes there are a million and one ingredients that come together to create the perfect impression. Anyone can do this. It's only a matter of desire and skill. And if the desire is there, the skills can be learned. In this book, I've collected the wisdom of many years, and the input of dozens of hosts and hostesses from all around the world. I hope it is an inspiration and a delight.

"For me, there is no greater pleasure than to invite people to my house. Entertaining is the way I express my love and friendship."

CHAPTER TWO

Setting the
Stage

IT'S ALL IN THE CARE YOU TAKE

Giving a party or hosting a dinner is in many ways like a performance. You are the producer, director, stage manager, and finally the actor. Dozens of details might go into the simplest occasion. A gifted hostess will always make her parties look effortless. As a friend once remarked, "I want my guests to feel as though I just walked through the door with them, ready to have a good time."

Think of the party as a drama and prepare to set the stage to perfectly suit the mood. The flowers, decor, and table settings are the props that will complete the picture. The right touches can make even the most casual parties stand out. I remember when I used to give barbecues. They were very informal. I served the favorite summer menu of steak, corn on the cob, and ice cream. But the setting was a dream. The hydrangeas were in bloom all around us, and I put little candles in the olive trees. I learned then that creating an ambience goes a long way toward making a successful party.

I want to share with you some of the nuts-and-bolts details of how I go about planning to entertain. I hope some of my tools and checklists will be helpful to you.

Every occasion has a purpose—whether it's out-of-town guests, a birthday, or simply the desire to see old friends. Naturally, the occasion determines what kind of party this will be.

I know hostesses whose greatest delight is to host a theme party. When we were young, Alfred and I used to do this too. Once we gave a Haunted House Party at Halloween. And in the early sixties, we gave a Twist Party, complete with Chubby Checker. I can still see the Hollywood columnists Hedda Hopper and Louella Parsons in their twirly twist dresses, dancing the night away.

I have a friend who is a self-admitted "chocoholic." Recently, she gave a Chocolate Lovers Party. Everything was chocolate, including the invitations, the decor, and all the food. Her guests were in heaven. Another friend hosted a Sixties Party in New York that was a lot of fun. Everyone went all-out—with big hairdos, bellbottoms—the works. One woman arrived with large pink curlers in her hair, covered with a scarf, the way some people used to do. Another came dressed as Jackie Kennedy, complete with pillbox hat. The hostess served a simple menu of hamburgers, fries, and ice cream sandwiches.

My friend Barbara Davis is known for her annual Valentine's Day luncheon. She hosts it at a local restaurant, but every detail is planned—right down to the red or pink dress each woman is asked to wear. All the food—including pasta, vegetables, and rolls—is heart-shaped. The table is set in red, white, and pink, with red, white, and pink flowers. And each guest is given a lovely thematic party favor; last year, it was a heart-shaped picture frame.

Theme parties are fun, and they're an instant icebreaker! But less dramatic occasions can also be spectacular.

The type of occasion determines where in the house you will be entertaining. Even if your house is not large, you can use your imagination to choose a space that might fit the mood of the party or be a little different. A small table set under a tree in the backyard makes for an intimate setting. A kitchen supper is fun and casual. My favorite place to entertain is the palm-shaded atrium that looks out over my garden. I usually decorate with pots of begonias, white geraniums, or other flowering plants. Flowers are the best way to add ambience. I love to do an arrangement of calla lilies in the front hallway. It's the first thing guests see when they walk into my house, and it's a conversation piece.

"Even if your house is not large, you can use your imagination to choose a space that might fit the mood of the party or be a little different."

Make a List

The first thing to do is sit down and make a list of all the details. This checklist helps you keep track. I always organize my checklists according to time, especially if it's a big party—what needs to be done a month ahead, two weeks ahead, days ahead, and on the day itself. It looks like this:

THINGS TO DO

1 month ahead
make guest list
invite guests
design the menu
arrange rentals (if needed)
arrange extra help (if needed)
select music (if appropriate)

2 weeks ahead
plan table settings
check, clean, and polish silver and
        tableware
select and press linens
check supplies (i.e. candles)

10 days ahead
send guest reminders (do this 2 weeks
        to 10 days ahead, and include
        details)
make shopping list

1 week ahead
final guest phoning
begin housecleaning
buy nonperishable food
buy wine and alcohol
write instructions for help

3 days ahead
buy meat, fish
begin preparing food
set the table (if possible)
finish housecleaning
diagram guest seating

| 2 days ahead | buy produce |
| | prepare food |

1 day ahead	cut or buy flowers and arrange
	prepare food
	write place cards

Make a Menu

I always take notes wherever I go, so over the years I've collected many menus. You'll find some of my favorites in Chapter Four. When I'm planning a menu, I start with the main course and build the other elements around it. A wise hostess will sometimes include a special recipe—a dish she is known for and her guests look forward to having.

It isn't necessary that all the food be home cooked. You might prepare one special dish and have the rest catered. Or prepare everything but the dessert yourself. I love to make my own desserts, but sometimes it's not possible. For example, last summer, when I gave my annual Fourth of July Party, there were fifty guests and two birthdays. I ordered four birthday cakes, and we pre-sliced two for passing immediately. It made things go much more smoothly.

When you're planning your menu, keep in mind the following criteria:

1. Create a menu around the senses—sight (color), smell, taste, texture.
2. Don't overwhelm your guests. If the main course is heavy, surround it with fresh, light vegetables and a light dessert.
3. Try serving a different course, something you think people might not have had before. Sometimes, I'll take a menu card from a party, and try to reproduce the dishes myself.

A menu need not always include a first, second, and third course. Feel free to experiment. Robin (Mrs. Angier Biddle) Duke, a great hostess, served a lunch of soup, quiche, and salad. The soup was served in a mug, and we ate from small trays on our laps. It was casual and fun and spirited. And the quiche was the best I ever tasted. I have another friend who was quite famous for her Sunday waffles. She put the waffle iron right in her living room, and the guests helped themselves.

Ann (Mrs. Kirk) Douglas told me about a vegetable theme dinner she attended that was quite a success. The first course was tomato soup, served in a head of lettuce cut like a bowl. The main course, a stew, was served in gourds of various sizes and shapes. Dessert was miniature hollowed-out pineapples filled with pineapple sherbet and raspberries.

Sometimes, especially for formal occasions, it's nice to make menu cards, which become lovely mementos of the occasion. Here is a sample of a menu card I received at the White House dinner honoring the Prince and Princess of Wales:

DINNER

Honoring
Their Royal Highnesses
The Prince and Princess of Wales

Lobster Mousseline
with Maryland Crab
Horseradish Sauce

Glazed Chicken Capsicum
Brown Rice
Garden Vegetables

Jicama Salad
Herbed Cheese
Croutons

Peach Sorbet Basket
Champagne Sauce
Petits Fours

Quail Ridge Chardonnay 1981
Conn Creek Cabernet Sauvignon 1979
Schramsberg Cuvée de Pinot 1982

THE WHITE HOUSE
Saturday, November 9, 1985

Guests—The Most Important Element

I have always said, "A great party is one where everyone is talking and no one is listening." Every hostess wants her guests to enjoy one another. That's why inviting guests is the most important part of making sure you have a successful party. I can't say it often enough: People make a party. You should take as much or more care with the guest list as with any other aspect of the occasion.

In this day and age, there is no longer a need to have boy-girl, boy-girl around your table. I, for one, am delighted to see that old custom ended. The obvious implication of inviting a man for every woman was that women could not be interesting, desirable guests unless they were paired with a man. We know that's not true! Today's guest list focuses on personality and creating the best mix, not on the sex of those invited. If there is a guest of honor, the list should be built around that individual. I like to include, as a rule of thumb, people of different ages. It seems to make for a more interesting party. And it doesn't hurt to throw in someone whose views are a bit controversial—as long as the person isn't too obnoxious. A party is never harmed by a little spice. If you're looking for an interesting guest, consider a professor at a nearby university or a local artist. They are natural conversation starters.

Unless it's a very formal occasion, I always invite by phone, then follow up with written reminders two weeks before the party. I must say, there is a tendency in this casual day and age for people to ignore the obligation to respond to invitations—even when they are provided with a stamped, return envelope. I don't think being casual is ever an excuse for being rude, but it happens, and this causes many headaches for hostesses. You can help eliminate this problem by using the phone and following up with written reminders.

If the occasion is formal or you want to send written invitations, there is a simple formula that may be used. Here are samples of invitations, properly worded, that I have received. Note that in many cases they are handwritten, often using calligraphy. The more personal you can make your invitations, the better. I think it's always a compliment when you write them yourself. It puts a little of your personal style into the inviting.

The following invitations show the correct format:

Mr. and Mrs. Fayez Sarofim
Norma S. Sarofim
and
Alexander P. Papamarkou
request the pleasure of the company of

Mrs. Betsy Bloomingdale
at dinner in honor of
H.E. the Secretary General
of the United Nations
and
Mrs. Boutros-Ghali

Monday, the ninth of March
seven-thirty o'clock
The Metropolitan Museum of Art
Fifth Avenue at Eighty-second Street
New York City

R.s.v.p.   Black tie
Ms. Anita Birchenall   7:30 cocktails
(212) 223-2020   8:30 dinner

Please present this invitation at the door.

"The more personal you can make your invitations, the better. I think it's always a compliment when you write them yourself."

MR. AND MRS. WALTER H. ANNENBERG

REQUEST THE PLEASURE OF

Mrs. Bloomingdale and Guest's

COMPANY   at dinner

ON   Tuesday, the thirty-first of December

AT   eight-fifteen   O'CLOCK Cocktails
              nine   o'clock Dinner

                              SUNNYLANDS
                              RANCHO MIRAGE, CALIFORNIA
R.S.V.P.
Black Tie

Here are two samples of reminder cards:

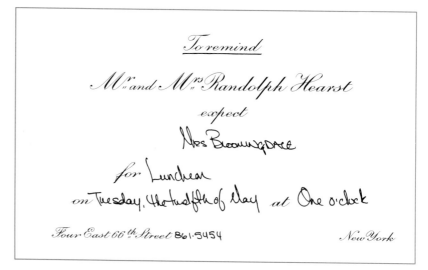

To remind

Mr. and Mrs. Randolph Hearst

expect

Mrs. Bloomingdale

for Luncheon

on Tuesday, the twelfth of May at One o'clock

Four East 66th Street 861-5454 New York

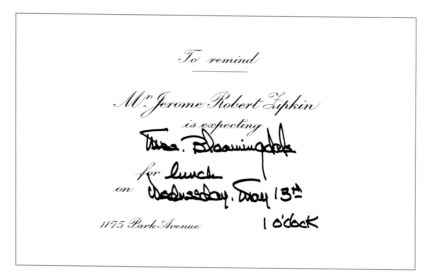

To remind

Mr. Jerome Robert Zipkin
is expecting

Mrs. Bloomingdale

for lunch

on Wednesday, May 13th

1175 Park Avenue 1 o'clock

Invitations can also be fun and original. Barbara Davis (of the Valentine Party mentioned earlier) is a master of this. Her invitations exceed all ordinary styles and are always incredible. They are events in and of themselves, arriving in small (and sometimes large!) boxes. For example, the invitation for one of her Christmas parties, described in Chapter Five, came in a 6-inch by 9-inch gold box. When you opened it, there was a heavy gold card to which was attached a miniature fireplace hung with stockings and a wreath. The inscription read, "A Storybook Holiday at the Knoll." Inside the card, along with the details of the party, there was a tiny switch. When you turned it on, the fireplace logs lit up, the wreath twinkled, and "Jingle Bells" played.

Some people send "save the date" cards, indicating they want you to plan to attend a party on a particular date, but do not yet have the details. Here is a sample from Lily and Edmond Safra. The invitation followed some time later.

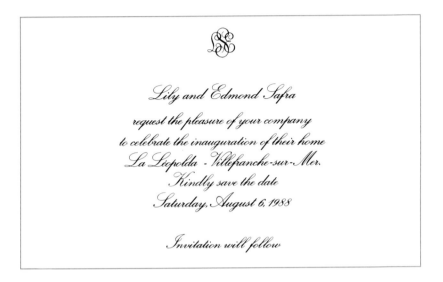

Lily and Edmond Safra

request the pleasure of your company
to celebrate the inauguration of their home
La Léopolda - Villefranche-sur-Mer.
Kindly save the date
Saturday, August 6, 1988

Invitation will follow

On your guest list, leave a space to check off those who have responded, so you can keep a running count as the weeks and days progress. You can't really make final preparations until you know how many people will be attending. If all goes well, you should have an accurate count at least a week before the party.

Of course, people being only human, you should always leave room for surprises. While it's a terrible breach of etiquette to bring along an uninvited guest, people nevertheless do it from time to time. Don't let it ruin your party. Have enough flexibility in your plans to set an extra place.

You might also encounter a situation where a guest becomes ill or is unable to attend at the last minute. If you've carefully planned your evening for eight, and don't want to be left with seven, you might quickly invite a replacement. I know many women would protest, "Oh, I can't possibly call someone at the last minute. They'll know they're just a fill-in. It would be too embarrassing." I disagree. Recently, I encountered just this situation. A friend's husband was ill, and she called the day before the party to tell me she was coming alone. I simply picked up the phone and called a single man I know and said, "Are you

doing anything tomorrow night?" He said no. I said, "Wonderful. I arranged to have a few people over and Susan's husband is ill. I'd love to have you in his place." He was delighted to be invited, and I didn't feel the least bit embarrassed to explain the reason. We all had a wonderful time.

Preparing Your Table

There are two important considerations when you're setting your table: First, does it achieve the look you want? And second, what is the best seating plan? Some hostesses have near nervous breakdowns trying to decide where to seat their guests. While it may be a challenge—especially if you've invited people you don't know well—there's no need to drive yourself crazy about it. It helps to keep in mind a few criteria:

1. Never seat husbands and wives together (although it is all right with engaged couples).
2. If you have more than one table, choose a "host" for each table.
3. If there is a guest of honor, seat a man on your right, and a woman on your husband or male host's right. (A president, past or present, sits on your right and a male guest of honor moves to your left.)
4. Try to mix people who know each other with new people to encourage lively conversation.

Naturally, no matter how carefully you seat your guests, you can't force them to be charming, witty, and attentive to their tablemates. That's up to them. My friend Jerome Zipkin tells of having an experience at a dinner he attended. The woman seated to his right spent the entire meal turned away from him, conversing with the person on her right. When the dessert was served, she finally looked over at him and said, "Oh, hello." Jerry, who can be acerbic and always says just what's on his mind, retorted, "I've been staring at your back all evening. Why stop now?"

The best guests are those who know that they too have a responsibility to make the party successful. They will go out of their way to be gracious and include those around them in their conversations. A friend who has taught me a great deal about how to be a perfect guest is Nancy Reagan. People often comment about what a wonderful listener she is—how interested she seems to be in each person. This quality is not something you can teach a person who doesn't already have it. Sometimes I wish good manners could be packaged and sold!

The table itself should be a work of art, reflecting your own taste and creativity. For a recent luncheon in the atrium, I used simple but dramatic tropical decor. The table was spread with a printed floral cloth. In the center, I placed a low, black lacquer bowl containing three four-inch needle frogs. Then I cut nine cyperus papyrus. Sometimes called Nile Grass, these are very long bamboo-like stems that shoot up at the top in a pompom umbrella effect. I placed three in each frog, at varying heights. Then I covered the frogs with lavender dahlias. The arrangement was striking and, most important of all, it didn't obstruct anyone's view of other guests. Decor should enhance, not take over, the table.

Happily, the old, rigid rules have given way to more fun and creative ideas. For example, I sometimes enjoy mixing and matching china with complementing patterns, rather than serving everything on the same pattern. It creates a colorful and eye-catching effect. Other times, I use the same service throughout.

Once I know who will be coming, I make a chart of my seating arrangements. Here is a sample chart I used for one of my dinners, held in honor of Governor Douglas Wilder of Virginia.

John Gavin

Judy Murphy	Ariana Huffington
Joe Hannan	Franklyn Murphy
Virginia Ramo	Connie Gavin
Dr. J. Billington	Si Ramo
Nancy Reagan	Pat Kluge
Governor Wilder	President Reagan

Me

For small, informal occasions, I just tell everyone where to sit. For more formal times, or with larger groups, I use place cards, writing with a heavy black felt-tipped pen so that people can find their places easily. There is a lot of debate about the "proper" way to write place cards. The correct form is:

FORMAL: Mr. Smith.
INFORMAL: Bill. If there is more than one Bill, add the first initial of the last name.

Going to Market

I make my shopping list early, and I like to spread the shopping out over several days—going to the supermarket one day, the meat market another, and so on. This is far less stressful than doing the shopping in one day, and it gives you time to make adjustments at the last minute.

The following is a sample shopping list for the menu on page 41. Some of the ingredients are staples in my house and there was no need to purchase them for this luncheon. But I've added them to the list to give you a complete picture. Notice I've divided the items according to category. The meat and fish are purchased one place, the bread another, and so on. Even if you do all your shopping at the supermarket, it helps to have an organized list.

SHOPPING LIST

MEAT/POULTRY MARKET
    2 large chicken breasts, boned

BAKERY
    various breads and rolls

PRODUCE STAND
    large bunch scallions   large onion
    fresh chives   3 lemons
    fresh tarragon   8 ripe peaches
    fresh parsley   4 large avocados
    2 large heads Belgian endive

DAIRY

    quart sour cream

    eggs

    margarine

BAKING SECTION

    cake flour

    confectioners' sugar

    granulated sugar

SPICE SECTION

    vanilla bean

    cream of tartar

    cumin

OTHER CANNED AND BOTTLED

    14-ounce can plum tomatoes

    two large cans chicken broth

    lemon juice

    capers

    Tabasco

    4-ounce can whole green chilies

    Dijon mustard

    red wine vinegar

    vegetable oil

    bottled water

    coffee

    tea

Wine

*C*alifornia has wonderful wines. My favorite for red and white is Jordan, but often for dinner I serve a California white and a French red.

The week before any party is a busy time. Be sure to pace yourself, taking care of a few details every day. If you do this, you will approach the day of the party with the energy and spirit to be full of fun and a perfect hostess for your guests.

CHAPTER THREE

The Pleasure of Your Company

A DANCE BETWEEN HOST AND GUEST

Everyone has been to a party where the hostess was so tired or so nervous that she gave people the jitters. Her distressed voice drifted out from the kitchen. Her face was pinched. She was so worried about pleasing her guests, she accomplished the opposite.

If you think about it, that's absurd. Since the reason for entertaining is to bring pleasure to people, there should never be any reason to let them see you upset or anxious. A relaxed hostess will make her guests feel relaxed.

Diana Vreeland, that great doyenne of style, once spelled out her secret to entertaining this way:

"Have a heart and care for your guests personally.

"Want them to come very much and give them each your attention.

"Save yourself for the event."

That is excellent advice, and the best way to follow it is to have everything done before the day of the party. Get a good night's sleep and rise early to finish any of the final details. Plan to spend most of the day on personal preparation—as though you are a guest attending your own party. If you have to rush to get ready at the last minute, you're not going to be very happy or calm. I've never known a woman (or a man, for that matter) who felt good about herself if she didn't have time to make sure she looked her best.

I take personal preparation very seriously. On the day of the party, when the last flower is arranged and the last detail is attended, I take a deep breath and relax. If I'm lucky and everything has been well planned in advance, I will have plenty of time to pamper myself. It is absolutely essential that a hostess refreshes herself, so she can emerge full of energy and eagerly looking forward to the occasion ahead—just like an invited guest.

If I can, perhaps I'll take a nap, or read and think about some current topics that might be conversation starters. I've put out my clothes in advance, and I spend as much time as I need getting ready. About a half hour before the guests are scheduled to arrive, I'll go downstairs and walk through the house, making one last check on the details.

When the doorbell rings, it's time to begin. Greet your guests at the door, putting your entire self into it, and making them feel glad to be there from the very first moment. Often, it takes some skill to get things moving. If one or two people arrive early, try not to leave them alone. Bring them with you into the kitchen if you're cooking yourself, or invite them to look at your garden or fix a drink.

Always introduce early arrivals to one another, and if they've never met, add a detail or two that will start them talking. A skilled hostess knows how to make this look natural.

When Calamity Strikes

A seasoned hostess understands that entertaining is a human endeavor and as such is filled with unexpected moments. Even the most perfectly executed parties can be marred by unexpected calamities. In my years of entertaining, I've certainly had my share.

Several years ago, I planned a dinner for twenty-six people. Although I don't normally do this, for that occasion I was using an outside cook to prepare the first course and main course, and I was making the hors d'oeuvres and dessert myself. The cook was preparing most of the food in his own kitchen and he planned to put on the finishing touches at my house.

My guests were scheduled to arrive at 7:30 PM, and at six o'clock I was all ready except for one thing: There was no sign of my cook. Seven o'clock came and went. Still no cook, and no answer on his phone. By then, it was beginning to occur to me that I had no dinner.

My first reaction was to panic for just a second. But I quickly pulled myself together and began to think about what I could do. I got on the phone and called a local restaurant that I frequent and implored the maitre d' to help me. I said to him, "I have twenty-six people arriving for dinner any minute, and there is no dinner."

He responded, "Oh, my! I'll have to see what I have twenty-six orders of and call you back."

Just at that moment, the cook arrived. It turned out that a man had tried to rob a local jeweler and held the employees captive. All of Beverly Hills was cordoned off and the freeway, a mess at rush hour anyway, was at a standstill. So was my dinner, which had been stuck on the freeway for two hours.

In the course of entertaining, calamities happen; food gets burned, sauce gets spilled, guests are late—or early. A friend of mine once had two of her dinner guests show up the night before the party. They had misread the date on the invitation. Of course, they were terribly embarrassed, but she responded graciously, invited them in for a drink, and made them feel completely at home. As they departed half an hour later, she told them how much she was looking forward to continuing their conversation the following evening. Another friend told of a woman who brought along an unexpected house guest, without calling ahead to ask if it would be all right. The event was a small dinner party of eight. My friend kept her unpleasant thoughts about this to herself, and cheerfully set another place at the table. And I'll never forget attending a dinner party where the cook became ill in the midst of preparation. Our hostess sent her off to lie down, and invited us into the kitchen to help her finish the meal. There was lots of fun and laughter and everyone had a wonderful time. It certainly broke the ice!

When Alfred started Diner's Club, we often entertained his business friends from all over the world. I was a nervous wreck because I was so afraid something would go wrong. But with time I learned that there is only one thing that can really ruin a party, and that is for the hostess to stop smiling. Everything else can be fixed.

"With time I learned that there is only one thing that can really ruin a party, and that is for the hostess to stop smiling."

Table Manners

If you're planning a seated dinner, you've already carefully arranged your seating to maximize the spirit of the group. But as the hostess, you must remain vigilant to the entire table, watching to be sure everyone is having a good time, getting enough to eat, and being included in conversation.

When there is more than one table, ask friends you trust to act as table hosts. I did this recently at my Fourth of July party. There were six tables, and I arranged for five people to play host at the other tables. When it was time to sit down, they gathered their groups to tell them where they were sitting, and they made sure everyone at the table was happy. It worked like a charm.

Every hostess has to contend at one time or another with a guest's nose being out of joint because of where he or she is seated. If you have a guest of honor, your first responsibility is to that person. Consider who he or she would like to sit with and go from there.

I prefer to serve by having the courses passed at the table. You or a helper can hold the platter while each guest takes what he or she wants. Or you can remain seated and pass the dish down the table. My least favorite method is plate service throughout a meal, where plates are prepared in the kitchen like in a restaurant. I do believe a first course can be plate service—for example, smoked salmon prettily arranged with avocado. But it's too impersonal for the entire meal, unless you're having a huge gathering. Even when I have others serving for me, I may have them give me a dish or the sauce and pass that myself. I'm always looking for the personal touches.

Lots of people do kitchen buffets, and I like to do them for family holiday leftovers. Simply lay out the food in the kitchen as you prepare it, and have people serve themselves.

Regarding the food, it probably goes without saying, but I'll say it anyway: Be sure that everyone has plenty. Dishes should be passed a second time when the guests have finished—especially the main course. Plan ahead for second helpings. Not everyone will want more, but you must make sure there is enough. This point is especially important if you are having a meal catered. Always order more than you think you'll need. Believe me, if the food is there, it will usually disappear. Also, if you serve wine with the meal, be sure everyone's glass is kept replenished. Or do as I sometimes do, and place wine bottles on the table so people can help themselves throughout the meal.

All of these small details add up to make your dinner pleasurable. You may appear to be deeply engaged in conversation with the person seated to your left or right, but in fact your attention is always focused on the entire table.

If you don't have someone helping, the menu should be such that you won't be spending too much of your time in the kitchen, or popping up and down from the table. Remember, when people are dining in your house, they've come to see you, and if you're busy in the kitchen throughout the meal, they'll feel disappointed and neglected.

I am always ready to spark the conversation if I see people are not talking. Part of a hostess's preparation is to be knowledgeable about current events. I'll always have a few conversation starters ready, based on the day's news. Or if a guest has done something special, I'll bring it to the attention of the table. I never leave anything to chance, and I'd rather have a lively political argument break out than have everyone quietly staring at their plates.

Although my fondest wish is that my guests will all take to one another immediately and engage in lively conversation from the beginning to the end of the evening, sometimes they need a little help.

My friends, who are accomplished hostesses themselves, know that the guests carry some of the responsibility. Many people, when they are invited to someone's house, think their only job is to show up. But guests have a responsibility, too, to be interesting and sociable. They should be considerate of the hostess, just as she is considerate of them. A party is like a dance between hostess and guests, with everyone contributing something to make it a success.

What if something goes wrong? My rule of thumb for spills and breakages is to look the other way. You may want to jump up in alarm as you see wine staining your favorite tablecloth, but it's more important to not embarrass your guest.

One thing that can really put a damper on a party is when a guest leaves early with a lot of fanfare. He or she may think it is polite to say goodbye to everyone, but I don't think it is if you're leaving early. The best way is to take "French leave." Just slip out quietly. When someone makes a big deal of saying good night, it

"What if something goes wrong? My rule of thumb for spills and breakages is to look the other way."

breaks up a party. Everyone else starts looking at their watches.

Recently, I had Kirk Douglas as a guest. Kirk will be the first to admit that he has a reputation for leaving parties early. Since he's an old friend, I felt I could say, "Go ahead and leave when you want to. Just don't say good night."

The greatest compliment to a hostess is when the guests are having such a good time they don't want to leave. However, every party must come to an end. If guests don't seem to be leaving, you can say, "I'm so glad you've had a good time, but I have to be up early in the morning." Sometimes, when my children's friends are here, they get involved in playing games late into the night. In that case, I just slip quietly upstairs and leave them to continue their fun.

As you see people to the door, you should be feeling very satisfied with the way things have gone. Don't start playing the evening over in your head, or dwelling on the minor mishaps and disappointments. Make a note of things you would change the next time. I always do. But if you've done your preparation, and made sure your guests knew how happy you were to have them there, your party has been a success.

In the following chapters, I will share wisdom, menus, and recipes from some of the best hosts and hostesses I know. They were all exceedingly generous in sharing with me. What stands out for me is that, in each and every case, they told me that the most important element of successful entertaining was not what you mixed up in the kitchen, but the mix of people at the table. The marvelous and original recipes they contributed are simply the "icing on the cake."

"If you've done your preparation, and made sure your guests knew how happy you were to have them there, your party has been a success."

CHAPTER FOUR

Creating Menu Magic

THE SECRET IS IMAGINATION

hen I give lectures to women's groups, the question that always comes up is how to design a perfect menu. Many people think there is a magic formula that tells you what's right, but really the secret is good organization. My friend Florence van der Kemp taught me that many years ago when she lived in the Palace of Versailles with her husband Gerald, then the curator. She was the first person I'd known to create a menu book. It included a variety of menus for all types of occasions, and she had reached the point where she could say to the cook, "We'll have Number Five for lunch tomorrow."

As far as knowing which foods go best together, the learning process is one of trial and error, with a liberal dose of imagination. I have always tested menus with my family before serving them to guests, and for the most part they never minded being the guinea pigs—although Alfred would sometimes say, "Oh, we're having this again?" Then, when I'd perfected it, he'd complain that it was the last time he ever saw it.

The menus in this chapter are an eclectic collection of my own favorites and those of my friends. They run the gamut from very casual to quite formal. I've chosen one or two—or sometimes more—recipes from each menu. They will give you some great new ideas for creating your own menu book.

MY OWN MENUS

Lunch in the Atrium
Light Summer Lunch
Favorite All-Season Lunch
Hot and Cold Winter Lunch
Evening Reception
Sunday Buffet
Satisfying Simple Supper
Informal Dinner
Formal Dinner
Alternate Formal Dinner

MENUS FROM FRIENDS

Buffet Luncheon
Palm Beach Lunch
Spring Luncheon
Light Lunch with Blockbuster Desserts
Afternoon Tea
Friday Buffet Supper
Sunday Night Supper Buffet
Outdoor Lunch in the Bahamas
Casual Dinner
Dinner in the Kitchen
Spring Dinner
Formal California Dinner
Formal New York Dinner
Formal Dinner in Rome
Jerry's Favorite Dinner
Southern Dinner
Spring Dinner for Margaret Thatcher

MY OWN MENUS

Lunch in the Atrium
M E N U

* Cold Avocado Soup with Tomato Ice
* Endive and Chicken Salad
Poached Peaches
* Family Sunshine Cake
Iced Mint Tea

Cold Avocado Soup with Tomato Ice

TOMATO ICE:

In a blender or a food processor fitted with a steel blade, purée the tomatoes and then the juice, and strain the purée through a fine sieve into a bowl, pressing hard on the solids. Add the stock, lemon juice, sugar, and Tabasco. Salt and pepper to taste.

Mix well and freeze in ice cube tray with dividers.

AVOCADO SOUP:

In a bowl, mash the avocados with the lemon juice and the cumin. Whisk in the hot broth and water. Mix well.

Strain the mixture through a fine sieve into a large bowl, pressing hard on the solids. Beat in the sour cream, and stir in the scallions and chilies. Salt and pepper to taste.

Chill the soup, covered, for about two hours or until it is cold. Ladle the soup into chilled bowls and put a slightly softened tomato ice cube in the center of each. Makes 8 servings.

TOMATO ICE:

1 can (14 ounces) Italian plum
   tomatoes, with juice
$1/2$ cup chicken stock or canned
   chicken broth
1 tablespoon fresh lemon juice
1 teaspoon sugar
$1/2$ teaspoon Tabasco
salt and pepper

AVOCADO SOUP:

4 very ripe avocados, pitted and
   peeled
6 tablespoons fresh lemon juice
$1^1/2$ teaspoons ground cumin
$4^1/2$ cups canned chicken broth,
   heated
$3/4$ cup water
$1/4$ cup sour cream
$1/2$ cup minced scallions
2 canned green chilies, chopped
salt and pepper

NOTE: Recipes are included for menu items marked with an asterisk (*).

Endive and Chicken Salad

2 large, boneless chicken breasts,
    cooked
2 large heads Belgian endive

SAUCE RAVIGOTE:
2 teaspoons Dijon mustard
1 tablespoon red wine vinegar
salt and pepper
$1/2$ cup vegetable oil
1 tablespoon drained capers
2 tablespoons finely chopped
    fresh parsley
2 tablespoons finely chopped
    onion
1 tablespoon finely chopped
    fresh chives
1 tablespoon finely chopped
    fresh tarragon

Cut the chicken into $1/2$-inch cubes to fill 4 measuring cups, and put it into a bowl.

Trim off the base of each endive. Pull off and reserve about 12 of the best outside endive leaves, to be used as garnish. Chop the remaining endive coarsely. There should be about $2^1/2$ cups. Add this to the chicken.

SAUCE RAVIGOTE:

Put the mustard, vinegar, salt, and pepper into a small mixing bowl. Add the oil gradually, stirring vigorously with a wire whisk. Add the capers, parsley, onion, chives, and tarragon. Blend well.

Pour the sauce over the chicken mixture and mix everything well. Place reserved endive leaves on plate or around edge of serving bowl. Place salad on leaves. Serve immediately. Serves 4. (Double if serving 8)

Family Sunshine Cake

1 teaspoon grated lemon zest
2 tablespoons lemon juice
2 tablespoons water
$1^1/2$ cups sugar, divided
6 eggs, separated, plus 1
    additional egg white
1 cup plus 2 tablespoons cake
    flour
$1/2$ teaspoon salt
$1/2$ teaspoon cream of tartar

LEMON ICING:
2 cups confectioners' sugar
$1/4$ cup butter or margarine, at
    room temperature
1 to 2 teaspoons water
1 lemon

Preheat oven to 350 degrees.

Blend lemon zest, juice, water, and 1 cup of sugar. Add egg yolks and beat until very light and fluffy. Sift together flour and remaining $1/2$ cup sugar 4 times. Blend flour-sugar mixture into yolk mixture.

Add salt to 7 egg whites and beat until foamy. Add cream of tartar and continue to beat until whites are stiff but not dry. Fold yolk mixture into whites. Do not overmix. Pour batter into a 10-inch tube pan and bake for 1 hour or until the cake springs back when lightly touched. Invert the pan and cool thoroughly before removing the cake.

Drizzle Easy Lemon Icing over the top.

EASY LEMON ICING:

Blend confectioners' sugar and butter or margarine. Beat in water. Grate zest from the lemon, then extract juice. Stir grated lemon zest and lemon juice into the sugar mixture. Makes about 1 cup of icing.

Light Summer Lunch
M E N U

*Avocado Salad with Warm Vinaigrette (recipe on page 168)

* Poached Salmon with Sauce Mousseline

Green Salad

Strawberries with Rind Sauce

* Erlinda's Orange Cake

Poached Salmon with Sauce Mousseline

Cut fillets into 2 pieces, bone, skin, and roll in a round shape; secure with a toothpick. Salt and pepper, and add a squeeze of lemon.

Place water in a large skillet and add the peppercorns, bay leaf, leek, scallions, and a little white wine.

Bring to a full boil and let boil for 5 minutes. Put in the salmon and turn off the heat. Cover and let sit for 5 minutes. Turn fish. Cover and let sit another 5 minutes. Salmon should turn dull-looking and flake. If not, cover and simmer for a few minutes. Remove salmon from water. Refrigerate both the water and salmon until needed.

Just before serving, remove the vegetables from the water and bring it to a boil again. Put salmon in for a few seconds to warm, if you have prepared it in advance.

Serve with Sauce Mousseline. Serves 6 to 8.

2 salmon fillets (about 12 ounces each)
salt and pepper
squeeze of fresh lemon juice
8 cups water
10 peppercorns
1 bay leaf
1 leek, sliced, green and all
2 scallions
a little white wine

SAUCE MOUSSELINE:

Reduce spinach or watercress to a purée, in a food processor or blender, and rub through a fine sieve. Mix with mayonnaise, blending it thoroughly. Whip heavy cream stiffly and add the mayonnaise very lightly. Serve in a sauce boat.

SAUCE MOUSSELINE:
2 handfuls spinach or watercress
1 cup mayonnaise
$1/2$ cup heavy cream

శ్రీ

Many of my recipes are the creation of Erlinda, who has been my cook for years. Like Lau before her, Erlinda loves to experiment and, since she's a natural cook, the result is always marvelous.

Erlinda's Orange Cake

1¼ cups sifted cake flour
1½ cups sugar, divided
8 egg whites
7 egg yolks
 grated zest of 2 oranges
4 tablespoons orange juice
½ teaspoon cream of tartar
1 teaspoon salt
confectioners' sugar

Preheat oven to 350 degrees.

Prepare a 10-inch, 2-piece tube pan. Grease bottom only, line with wax paper, then grease lightly again. Do not grease the sides of the pan.

Sift flour and ½ cup of sugar 4 times.

In a medium mixing bowl, combine the orange juice and zest. Beat in the remaining 1 cup of sugar and mix well. Beat in the egg yolks and continue beating until light in color. Add the flour mixture, 2 tablespoons at a time, until light in color and mixture is smooth. Set aside.

In another large mixing bowl, beat the egg whites with salt until frothy, then add the cream of tartar and beat until stiff but not dry. Be careful to beat only until stiff peaks form when the beater is raised slowly.

Put ⅓ of the egg white mixture into the batter and mix well with a clean wooden spoon. With a rubber spatula, gently fold in the remaining egg whites. Pour half the mixture in the pan and level with the rubber spatula. Pour the remaining mixture in the pan, level again, then bounce the tube pan on a hard surface 3 times to remove air pockets. Bake 50 minutes to 1 hour.

The cake is done when a cake tester inserted in the center comes out clean and the cake springs back when lightly pressed. The center will rise above the pan when baking and sink slightly when done.

Invert the pan immediately and support the tube on a funnel or bottle. Cool the cake completely in the pan.

Loosen the sides and the center core with a metal spatula or a thin, sharp knife. Avoid any up-and-down motion. Invert onto a serving plate.

Sprinkle with confectioners' sugar sifted through a fine strainer in a decorative way. Slice the cake thinly with a warm knife, wetting the knife with water every time you slice. Serves 10 to 12.

Favorite All-Season Lunch
M E N U

* Chiles Rellenos
* Crab Cakes Around Corn Pudding
Red Potato, Cherry Tomato, String Bean Salad
Caramel Soufflé
Stem Strawberries

Chiles Rellenos

Split whole chilies lengthwise and lay flat in the bottom of a 13 x 9-inch pan. Mix cheeses together. Top chilies with half of the cheese. Sprinkle with diced chilies, and top with remaining cheese.

Beat together the eggs and evaporated milk, and pour over the chili-cheese mixture. Bake at 350 degrees for 30 to 35 minutes. Let stand 10 minutes before serving. Serves 6.

Crab Cakes Around Corn Pudding

TO MAKE CRAB CAKES:
Whisk the eggs, then add mayonnaise, mustard, lemon juice, salt, and cayenne pepper. After mixing well, add the crabmeat and the fresh bread crumbs. Shape the mixture into eight 1-inch thick patties.

Coat patties lightly with dry bread crumbs. Cover with plastic and refrigerate for 1 hour. Melt butter in the oil in a heavy nonstick skillet over medium heat. Add crab cakes and cook until golden—3 to 4 minutes per side. Serves 6 to 8.

TO MAKE CORN PUDDING:
Grease a 2-quart timbale mold.
Beat eggs, then add remaining ingredients. Mix well. Pour into the mold and bake at 400 degrees for 20 minutes. Turn oven down to 350 degrees and continue cooking for 1 hour and 25 minutes or until golden brown.

CHILES RELLENOS:
1 can (7 ounces) whole green chilies
1 pound Monterey jack cheese, shredded (4 cups)
1 pound sharp cheddar cheese, shredded (4 cups)
1 can (7 ounces) diced green chilies
8 eggs
1 can (12 ounces) evaporated milk

CRAB CAKES:
2 large eggs
3 tablespoons mayonnaise
1 tablespoon Dijon mustard
2 tablespoons fresh lemon juice
$\frac{1}{2}$ teaspoon salt
$\frac{1}{4}$ teaspoon cayenne pepper
1 pound lump crabmeat, flaked
$\frac{1}{2}$ cup fresh bread crumbs
$\frac{1}{3}$ cup plain, dry bread crumbs
3 tablespoons butter
2 tablespoons vegetable oil

CORN PUDDING:
6 large eggs
3 cups fresh corn off the cob
$\frac{2}{3}$ cup bread crumbs, packed lightly to measure
3 tablespoons grated onion
$\frac{1}{2}$ cup chopped fresh parsley
$\frac{2}{3}$ cup grated cheese (mix cheddar and Gruyère)
$\frac{2}{3}$ cup heavy cream
1 teaspoon salt
8 grinds white peppercorn
8 drops Tabasco

Hot and Cold Winter Lunch
M E N U

* Tortellini
Chicken with Two Sauces
Cold Vegetable Platter
Sliced Oranges
* Poppyseed Cake

ॐ

I often like the idea of serving a hot first course, followed by a cold main course—even in winter. In this menu, the tortellini is hot and the chicken is cold.

Tortellini

Bring 4 quarts of water to a boil. Add a dash of salt.

Heat the oil in a skillet and add the onion and garlic. Cook until wilted, then add the ham and cook, stirring, for about 1 minute. Add the zucchini and continue to cook, stirring, for another minute. Add the tomatoes and cook for 5 minutes.

Meanwhile, put the tortellini in the boiling water and cook 5 to 8 minutes or until done. Remove and drain, reserving $1/4$ cup of cooking liquid.

Add the cooking liquid to the tomato mixture, along with the cream and cheese. Stir well. Add the tortellini and blend well. Sprinkle with scallions and serve. Serves 4.

Poppyseed Cake

Preheat oven to 325 degrees.

Measure and sift together in a mixing bowl the flour, sugar, baking powder, and salt. Make a well in the dry ingredients and add cooking oil, egg yolks, sherry, and vanilla. Beat well with a spoon until smooth.

In another bowl, whip egg whites with cream of tartar until they form stiff peaks. Do not underbeat as this must be much

TORTELLINI:
3 tablespoons olive oil

$1/2$ cup finely chopped onions

1 tablespoon finely minced garlic

$1/2$ pound cooked ham, cut into small cubes

$1/2$ pound zucchini, cut into small cubes

$1^{1}/4$ pounds tomatoes, peeled and cut into cubes

1 package (9 ounces) tortellini

$1/2$ cup heavy cream

2 tablespoons grated Parmesan cheese

$1/2$ cup finely chopped scallions

POPPYSEED CAKE:
$2^{1}/4$ cups sifted cake flour

$1^{1}/2$ cups sugar

3 teaspoons baking powder

1 teaspoon salt

$1/2$ cup vegetable oil

5 egg yolks, unbeaten

$3/4$ cup sherry

2 teaspoons vanilla

1 cup egg whites (7 or 8)

$1/2$ teaspoon cream of tartar

$1/2$ cup poppyseeds

confectioners' sugar

stiffer than for angel food. Pour flour and egg yolk mixture gradually over whipped egg whites, gently folding with a rubber scraper until the mixture is just blended. Do not stir. Gently fold in poppyseeds. Pour into an ungreased 10-inch tube pan immediately. Bake for 65 minutes.

Remove pan and immediately invert, resting edges of the pan on two other pans. Allow to hang until cold. Loosen from sides of the pan with a spatula. Turn pan over and hit edge sharply to loosen. Sprinkle with sifted confectioners' sugar. Serves 16 to 20.

Evening Reception
M E N U

* Lolly Pops
Bologna Wedges
* Guacamole Cups
* Peanut Butter and Bacon
* Onion Puffs
* Bacon Waverly
Crudités
Nuts
Oriental Pecans
Endive Fingers

Lolly Pops

Spread thin ham slices with soft cream cheese that has been mixed with seasoned salt. Put a sweet pickle in the center of each and roll tight like a jelly roll. Cut off the ends. Cover with clear wrap and chill. Slice thin to serve. Put toothpicks on the side—thus the name.

Guacamole Cups

Take thin white bread and roll flat with a rolling pin. Butter both sides lightly. Cut into rounds to fit into a small muffin pan and bake until light brown. Fill with guacamole.

Peanut Butter and Bacon

These are the most popular appetizers I've ever served. They always fly off the tray.

Fry bacon until crisp. Sauté thin white bread rounds in the fat remaining in the pan. Drain on paper towels. Spread peanut butter on the rounds. Sprinkle with crumbled bacon.

Onion Puffs

ONION PUFFS:
1 cup mayonnaise
1 finely chopped green onion
dry toast rounds
3 tablespoons grated Parmesan
    cheese

Mix together mayonnaise and onion and place on top of toast rounds. Sprinkle with Parmesan cheese and broil.

Bacon Waverly

Cut bacon slices in halves. Separate Waverly crackers at the perforations. Wrap a bacon half around the center of each cracker and sprinkle lightly with brown sugar. Place on a broiler rack, seam side down, over a drip pan. Bake at 350 degrees for 20 to 25 minutes or until the bacon is crisp.

Sunday Buffet
M E N U

* Erlinda's Oxtail
Chicken Breast with Apples
Florets of Cauliflower and Broccoli
*Jalepeño Cornbread
Mixed Green Salad
Apple Crisp

❧

Some people are put off by the idea of oxtail, but it's quite delicious—especially when Erlinda prepares it. I've been known to let people think it's a veal knuckle, and then when they rave about it, I admit the truth. They're always amazed and want the recipe.

Erlinda's Oxtail

Preheat oven to 450 degrees.

Wash and pat dry the meat. Season lightly with salt and pepper. Dredge the meat with the flour, and shake to remove excess.

In a large, heavy skillet heat oil until hot but not smoking; sauté the meat, 8 to 10 pieces at a time, until it's lightly brown on both sides. Don't overlap. Add more oil if necessary. Drain and pat dry. Set aside.

In a Dutch oven or a large, deep nonstick skillet over high heat, add the onions and garlic and cook, stirring often, until they are translucent—about 5 minutes. Add the carrots and cook for 5 minutes more. Add the meat and thyme. Mix well with the vegetables. Pour in the liquid mixture (consommé, tomato, and vegetable juice). It should lightly cover the meat. Boil gently on top of the stove, mix, cover, and transfer to the preheated oven. Cook for 1 hour.

Reduce oven to 400 degrees. After 30 minutes, mix again and remove 4 cups of the sauce to a medium, heavy saucepan. Let it sit on top of the stove.

Cook the meat for another 30 minutes, adding a little water if necessary. Season with salt and pepper. The total cooking time is 2 to 2½ hours.

Remove floating fat from the separate sauce with a spoon. Simmer the sauce, stirring often, until it is slightly thickened.

Before serving, transfer the meat to a heated platter, pour some of the hot sauce on top, and sprinkle with parsley. Serve the remainder of the sauce separately—very hot and sprinkled with parsley. Serves 20 to 30.

40 pieces oxtail
salt and pepper
flour
4 tablespoons vegetable oil
2 large onions, finely chopped
1 clove garlic, finely chopped
2 cups finely chopped carrots
2 tablespoons dried thyme, crumbled
4 cups beef consommé
2 cups tomato juice
2 cups V-8 juice
1 cup finely chopped fresh parsley

Jalapeño Corn Bread

Preheat oven to 375 degrees.

Combine all ingredients in order listed, and mix well. Put in well-greased 9 x 13-inch baking pan and bake for 45 minutes to 1 hour.

3 cups corn bread mix
2½ cups milk
3 eggs
3 teaspoons sugar
½ cup vegetable oil
1 can (16 ounces) creamed corn
½ cup finely chopped Jalapeño pepper (see note)
1½ cup grated cheddar cheese
½ cup grated onions

Note: When preparing fresh chilies, wear rubber gloves for protection against oils that later can cause a burning sensation on skin.

Satisfying Simple Supper
M E N U

Borscht à la Russe
* Sweet Pepper Pork
* Prune Soufflé with Custard Sauce

2 tablespoons vegetable oil
2 boneless tenderloins of pork
    (³/₄ to 1 pound each)
salt and pepper to taste
¹/₂ teaspoon paprika
¹/₂ cup finely chopped onion
¹/₂ cup finely chopped garlic
¹/₄ cup dry white wine
1 bay leaf
¹/₂ cup beef broth
¹/₄ teaspoon dried thyme
2 large sweet red peppers—
    cored, seeded, deveined
2 tablespoons sour cream
2 tablespoons heavy cream
2 tablespoons chopped parsley

PRUNE SOUFFLE:
1 pound dried prunes (2¹/₂ cups)
hot water
5 egg whites
¹/₈ teaspoon salt
¹/₄ teaspoon cream of tartar
¹/₂ cup sugar
1 teaspoon grated lemon zest
¹/₂ cup broken nut meats
    (optional)

Sweet Pepper Pork

Heat the oil in a heavy skillet until it is quite hot. Salt and pepper the tenderloins and sprinkle with paprika. Add the tenderloins to the skillet. Cook to brown evenly on all sides. Pour off the fat and place the onions and garlic around the meat. Cook for 4 minutes, then add the wine, bay leaf, broth, and thyme. Bring to a boil, stirring constantly, then cover tightly and cook for 15 minutes.

Cut the peppers into thin strips. Add them to the meat after it has cooked for 15 minutes, then continue cooking for 5 more minutes.

Move meat to a platter. Add sour cream and heavy cream to the skillet and stir it to blend. Remove bay leaf and pour the sauce over meat. Sprinkle with parsley. Serves 4 to 6.

Prune Soufflé with Custard Sauce

Cover prunes with hot water and soak for 1 hour. Bring to boiling point. Reduce heat and simmer gently for about 20 to 30 minutes or until prunes are soft and mushy. Drain and pit stewed prunes, then put them through a ricer. There should be 1 cup of thick prune pulp.

Preheat oven to 350 degrees.

Whip the egg whites and salt until foamy. Then add the cream of tartar and whip until stiff. Fold in the sugar and the prune pulp. Then fold in the lemon zest, and nuts if desired.

Place the soufflé in a 9-inch baking dish. Set it in a pan of hot water. Bake for about 1 hour or until it is firm. Serve hot or cold (I prefer hot) with custard sauce. Equally good with dried apricots. Serves 4 to 6.

CUSTARD SAUCE:

Beat the egg yolks well, then beat in the confectioners' sugar gradually. Add the vanilla.

Whip the heavy cream until it's stiff. In a separate bowl, whip the egg whites until stiff. Fold cream into the yolk mixture, then fold in egg whites.

See **Egg Caution note in the appendix, page 188.

CUSTARD SAUCE:
2 egg yolks
1 cup confectioners' sugar
1 1/2 teaspoons vanilla or 2 tablespoons brandy
1 cup heavy cream
2 egg whites

M E N U

Endive and Beet Salad
* Texas Meat Loaf
Baked Potatoes
* Peachy Ice Cream (recipe on page 186)

Texas Meat Loaf

Combine the ground beef and pork in a bowl. In a separate bowl, beat the eggs, then stir in the milk and rolled oats. Add this mixture to the meat and mix thoroughly.

Add the Worcestershire sauce, tomatoes, celery, onion, green pepper, salt, pepper, and spices, and mix thoroughly. Press into an oval roasting pan and lay the bacon strips on top. Bake at 425 degrees for 50 minutes. Serves 6.

MEAT LOAF:
1 pound lean ground beef
1/2 pound ground pork
2 eggs
1 cup milk
1/2 cup rolled oats
1/4 cup Worcestershire sauce
1/2 cup canned tomatoes, drained and chopped
1/2 cup diced celery
1/2 cup diced onion
1/2 cup diced green pepper
1/4 teaspoon salt
1 teaspoon pepper
1 teaspoon dried basil
1 teaspoon dried thyme
1/2 teaspoon dried oregano
1 clove garlic, minced
5 slices bacon

Formal Dinner
MENU

Poached Salmon
* Lamb Medallions with Mushrooms
* Potatoes Dauphinoise (recipe on page 175)
String Beans
Eggplant
* Best Vanilla Ice Cream
* Chocolate Sauce

Lamb Medallions with Mushrooms

2 racks of lamb, about 4¹/₂ pounds
3 teaspoons vegetable oil, divided
¹/₂ pound mushrooms, cut into quarters
salt and pepper
2 tablespoons butter, divided
2 teaspoons finely minced garlic

Cut away the meaty eyes of each rack and cut each eye in half crosswise, or diagonally if you prefer. Set aside.

Heat 1 teaspoon of oil and add mushrooms and salt and pepper to taste. Cook, stirring, until mushrooms give up liquid. Continue cooking, shaking and stirring, until mushrooms are browned and free of liquid. Set aside.

Heat remaining 2 teaspoons of oil in a heavy skillet large enough to comfortably hold lamb in one layer. Add lamb and sprinkle with salt and pepper. Cook over moderately high heat for about 2 minutes or until lamb is browned on one side. Turn meat and cook the other side—a total of about 8 minutes. Pour off fat and add 1 tablespoon of butter. Continue cooking, turning meat in butter, for about 30 seconds.

Heat mushrooms and add the remaining 1 tablespoon butter and the garlic. Cook briefly, shaking and stirring.

Arrange lamb slices and pour mushroom mixture over the top. Spoon on butter in which lamb was cooked. Serves 4.

❧

I always serve this in a wonderful mold I bought years ago in Vienna. It is made just for ice cream or soufflé glace, and has a screw-on top that you unscrew to release the air and ice cream. I place it on a 1¹/₂-inch-thick round of ice to make a grand presentation.

Best Vanilla Ice Cream

Beat egg yolks until light. Add sugar and continue to beat until very smooth and very light in color.

Pour in heavy cream. Add vanilla extract and beat with a rotary beater until well blended.

Freeze according to your ice cream maker directions. Makes about 1 quart.

**See Egg Caution note in the appendix, page 188.

6 egg yolks
1 1/2 cups sugar
4 cups heavy cream
2 tablespoons vanilla

This is the most fabulous chocolate sauce; make plenty because it's almost every man's favorite. I've guarded this recipe for years—now here it is.

Chocolate Sauce

Melt butter in the top of a double boiler over simmering water. Stir in sugar and evaporated milk. Add chocolate. Let stand over simmering water, without stirring, for 1/2 hour. Remove from heat and beat the sauce with an electric beater. Add vanilla to taste. You may wish to add a pinch of salt. This sauce can be thinned with half-and-half if you prefer it less thick.

1/4 pound plus 4 tablespoons (1 1/2 sticks) butter
2 1/4 cups confectioners' sugar
2/3 cup evaporated milk (1 small can)
6 squares unsweetened chocolate
1 teaspoon vanilla, about
salt (optional)

Alternate Formal Dinner
MENU

* Sorrel Soup
Linda's Whole Stuffed Chicken
Lau's Crispy Potatoes
Mixed Miniature Vegetables
Asparagus Diced on the Diagonal
Endive Salad
* Peggy's Bread-and-Butter Pudding with Lemon Sauce

Sorrel Soup

2 tablespoons butter
6 scallions, finely chopped
3 generous handfuls fresh sorrel
salt and pepper
2 tablespoons flour
7 cups chicken stock, boiling
2 egg yolks
1 cup heavy cream
buttered croutons

In a heavy pan, bring butter to a foaming stage and add scallions. Cook until soft but not brown. Add sorrel and salt and pepper to taste, then cover pan, cooking slowly for 5 minutes. Mix thoroughly. Sprinkle flour over the mixture and mix it thoroughly. Stir in stock and cook a few minutes more.

Run mixture through a strainer or blend in a blender. Return the purée to the pan and heat until it's simmering.

In a bowl, beat egg yolks and cream together, and dribble into the hot soup, stirring constantly. The soup may be served hot or cold. When ready to serve, sprinkle buttered croutons on top of each cup. Serves 6.

જીજ

Peggy Bolton was a longtime family friend who had a knack for cooking. You'd think by the dinners she served that she had a staff in the kitchen, but she did everything herself. We always looked forward to her Bread-and-Butter Pudding. Though not a formal dessert, I find it a great favorite anytime, and this is the best recipe.

Peggy's Bread-and-Butter Pudding With Lemon Sauce

PUDDING:
shortening
cinnamon bread, buttered
3 eggs
1/2 cup sugar
1/4 teaspoon salt
1 quart milk
raisins
ground cinnamon
ground nutmeg

LEMON SAUCE:
3 egg yolks
5 1/3 tablespoons butter
1 cup sugar
3 tablespoons lemon juice
grated zest of 1 lemon
1/3 cup boiling water

Preheat oven to 325 degrees.

Grease a 2-quart casserole with shortening and fill it to 1 inch from the top with thickly buttered cinnamon bread, butter side down. Using a fork, mix together slightly beaten eggs, sugar, salt , milk, and raisins. Pour this mixture over the bread and let stand for 30 minutes. Bake for 1 hour, covering for the first half hour. Sprinkle with cinnamon and nutmeg and serve with Lemon Sauce. Serves 8.

LEMON SAUCE:

Beat egg yolks with a fork; combine in top of double boiler with butter, sugar, lemon juice, zest, and water. Cover and cook over low heat until thickened.

MENUS FROM FRIENDS

Buffet Luncheon

FROM PRINCE RUPERT LOEWENSTEIN

Prince Rupert, who is best known as the banker for the Rolling Stones, is accustomed to entertaining in grand fashion at home in England. I will never forget the magnificent ball he gave to celebrate the twenty-first birthday of his son Conrad, which was attended by five hundred guests. But what Rupert and his wife Josephine enjoy the most are the buffet luncheons around the pool at their house in Los Angeles. Prince Rupert said that in Los Angeles "the clothes are as casual as they are formal for a ball in England where, as you may remember, many men wore white tie and tails, and all the ladies wore long dresses and some of the more fortunate ones wore tiaras."

When asked what is the most important element in entertaining, he thought carefully before answering. He feels that the answer is different in different countries.

"The real mark of a great host or hostess is that he or she must make every guest, however modest, feel welcomed and at ease. Even an overcooked filet might be forgiven in France, and a crashing bore forgotten in England, if every guest feels that the host or hostess is actively concerned with his well-being."

Prince Rupert described his buffet luncheons this way: "At our buffet luncheons in Los Angeles we normally have between twelve and twenty-four people sitting at two or three round tables under large white umbrellas.

"The tables are set only with the knives, forks, and glasses, and with carafes of white wine (Grgich Hills Chardonnay 1988) and Evian water.

"Usually, the buffet will contain one hot dish and two principal cold ones. Once they are cleared, there will be desserts. Before lunch, there are simple canapés and a wide variety of drinks. Although the recipes are all traditional, they have been modified and subtly improved by our two wonderful cooks, Miss Midge May in Los Angeles and Miss Jacqueline Rose in London."

Buffet Luncheon
M E N U

*Parmesan Cookies

Freshly squeezed grapefruit juice

Juice of Meyers lemons and oranges

Champagne (Bollinger 1985)

Bloody Marys with a base of Mrs. Gooch's tomato juice

and Mrs. Gooch's spicy vegetable juice

Kedgeree

* Risotto

* Vitello Tonnato

Sea Bass with a Cold Dill & Sour Cream Sauce

Spinach & Bacon Salad

Lemon Squares

Sacher Torte

Chocolate Mousse

Pink Grapefruit Sorbet

* Black Currant Sorbet

Parmesan Cookies

1 pound grated Parmigiano-
   Reggiano cheese (5$\frac{1}{3}$ cups)
$\frac{1}{2}$ pound butter (2 sticks), at
   room temperature
12 ounces flour (2$\frac{2}{3}$ cups)
salt and pepper

Mix cheese, butter, flour, and salt and pepper to taste, together. Form into round logs, approximately 1$\frac{1}{2}$ inches in diameter. Wrap in plastic and chill for at least 3 hours.

Preheat oven to 375 degrees.

To cook, slice into coin shapes $\frac{1}{4}$ inch thick and bake for 10 to 12 minutes until golden. Serve warm. Makes 50 cookies.

Risotto

Heat olive oil in a large, heavy-based saucepan. Cook the shallots for a few minutes, then stir in rice. Continue stirring over low heat and gradually add stock, a ladleful at a time. After about 20 minutes, it will start thickening. It is important to add stock only when the rice has absorbed liquid already in the pan. The consistency needs to be thick but sloppy. Next add the mushrooms and continue to stir. Add more stock as needed. About 10 minutes before the end, stir in the asparagus, Parma ham, and saffron. Season with salt and pepper.

Just before serving, mix in Parmesan cheese. Serves 8.

RISOTTO:

5 tablespoons olive oil

4 shallots, chopped

10 ounces arborio rice (about $1\frac{1}{3}$ cups)

4 to 6 cups chicken stock

$\frac{1}{2}$ pound mushrooms, cut into quarters

$\frac{3}{4}$ pound asparagus tips, cooked

3 thick slices Parma ham, chopped

$\frac{1}{2}$ ounce saffron, in white wine

salt and pepper

4 ounces grated Parmesan cheese (about $1\frac{1}{3}$ cups)

Vitello Tonnato

Cover veal with lots of bacon and roast for about $1\frac{1}{2}$ hours at 350 degrees. It must be rare. Remove from the oven and refrigerate to chill completely.

SAUCE:

Place the tuna, anchovy, capers, and lemon juice in a blender until smooth. Add mayonnaise. Continue blending, adding olive oil slowly. Refrigerate until needed.

When veal is completely cold, remove bacon and slice veal very thinly. Arrange on a large plate and spoon the sauce over. Decorate with capers and anchovy fillet. Serves 10.

VEAL:

3 pound joint very young veal fillet

bacon

SAUCE:

1 can ($6\frac{1}{4}$ ounces) tuna fish

4 anchovy fillets, plus more for garnish

3 tablespoons capers, plus more for garnish

1 lemon, juice only

$1\frac{1}{2}$ cups mayonnaise

$\frac{3}{4}$ cup olive oil

Black Currant Sorbet

Gently cook the black currants until their skins burst. Purée them and pass through a sieve, discarding the pulp. Add water to make 1 pint of purée, and pour into a saucepan. Add the sugar and fold in the beaten egg white. Heat gently to allow sugar to dissolve.

Allow to cool. In the meantime, start chilling the ice cream machine. Pour in cool mixture, turn on paddle, and mix for 40 to 50 minutes, until thick and smooth. Freeze until needed. Serves 6.

SORBET:

1 pound black currants

8 ounces sugar (1 cup plus 2 tablespoons)

1 egg white, beaten until stiff

Palm Beach Lunch

FROM CHANDLER COX MASHEK

*C*han Mashek is a wonderful young hostess who is one of the most organized people I've ever met. She makes her parties seem effortless. She credits the imaginative and healthy menus to her chef, John Balmer—especially this perfect Palm Beach luncheon.

M E N U

* Tomato Ice
* Rice Popovers
Artichoke Crab Salad
Marinated Vegetables
* Mango Mousse

TOMATO ICE:

6 large tomatoes, peeled, seeded, and chopped

$^1/_2$ cup chopped onion

$^1/_2$ cup chopped celery

$1^1/_2$ tablespoons sugar

$1^1/_2$ tablespoons fresh lemon juice

$^3/_4$ teaspoon Worcestershire sauce

$^1/_2$ teaspoon salt

3 to 4 drops Tabasco

2 small crushed garlic cloves

4 sprigs fresh mint (garnish)

Tomato Ice

Combine tomatoes, onion, celery, sugar, lemon juice, Worcestershire sauce, salt, Tabasco, and garlic in a blender or food processor and purée until smooth. Taste and adjust seasonings (should be highly seasoned). Pour into a shallow container and freeze.

Spoon mixture into processor and mix until fluffy (or transfer to medium bowl and beat with electric mixer). Return to container, cover, and freeze until firm. Serve in soup bowls garnished with mint sprigs. Serves 4 to 6.

POPOVERS:

1 cup all-purpose flour

1 tablespoon sugar

$^1/_4$ teaspoon salt

$^1/_2$ cup cooked rice

1 egg

2 egg whites

1 cup 2 percent low-fat milk

vegetable-oil cooking spray

Rice Popovers

Preheat oven to 450 degrees.

Combine flour, sugar, and salt, and set aside. Mash rice in a bowl with a potato masher. Add egg and egg whites, stirring with a whisk until well blended. Add flour mixture and milk alternately to rice mixture, beginning and ending with flour mixture, stirring with a whisk after each addition.

Heat muffin pans in the oven for 3 minutes; coat with cooking spray. Divide batter among pans. Bake for 15 minutes; reduce heat to 350 degrees and bake for 20 minutes. Cool in pans for 3 minutes. Yield: 12 popovers. About 70 calories each.

Mango Mousse

Combine mangos, lime juice, and sugar in a food processor and purée until liquid. Whip heavy cream to stiff whipped cream and fold into base.

Put salt in egg white and whip to stiff peaks and fold into above mixture. Let mousse chill overnight and serve in chilled hollow oranges. Serves 4 to 6.

See **Egg Caution note in the appendix, page 188.

3 medium mangos or 1 pound of
   pulp
2 tablespoons lime juice
2 egg whites
pinch of salt
4 tablespoons sugar
$1/2$ cup heavy whipping cream

Spring Luncheon

FROM DEEDA (MRS. WILLIAM MCCORMICK) BLAIR

I've known the lovely, impeccably dressed Deeda for years. Her husband Bill was ambassador to the Philippines and Denmark, and today they make their home in Washington, D.C., where Deeda is very involved working for cancer and AIDS. The Blairs entertain often and always have interesting guests. This luncheon is a standby for summer days.

M E N U

Cold Cooked and Fresh Vegetables
Lobster Salad
* Pasta Soufflé
* Green Grape Sorbet

Pasta Soufflé

BECHAMEL SAUCE:

1¹/₂ cups milk

3 tablespoons butter

4 tablespoons flour

¹/₄ teaspoon salt

SOUFFLE:

2 scant (not quite full) cups
   béchamel sauce

1 cup heavy cream

8 ounces angel hair pasta or
   linguini

1 cup freshly grated Parmesan
   cheese

4 tablespoons butter

6 egg yolks, slightly beaten

7 to 8 egg whites

freshly ground black pepper

BECHAMEL SAUCE:

Bring milk to a boil in a small saucepan over medium heat. Meanwhile, melt butter in a small, heavy saucepan over low heat. Add flour and cook, stirring constantly with a wire whisk for 1 to 2 minutes. Do not let flour brown.

Remove from heat. Add milk all at once, stirring vigorously with the whisk to prevent lumps from forming. Add salt and stir. Return pan to the burner and cook the sauce for a few minutes longer, stirring constantly until it is thick, smooth, and creamy.

FOR THE SOUFFLE:

Preheat oven to 375 degrees.

Add the cream to the béchamel and cook over low heat for 1 to 2 minutes. Remove from heat.

Drop the pasta into 2 to 3 quarts of boiling salted water. If the pasta is fresh, cook 2 minutes; if frozen, cook 4 minutes. Drain. Add the pasta, Parmesan cheese, and butter to the béchamel and stir well. Stir in the egg yolks and the pepper and taste for salt.

Butter an 8-cup soufflé dish. Whip the egg whites until stiff but not dry. Fold them into the pasta mixture. Pour the mixture into the soufflé dish. Bake for 40 minutes. Serves 6 to 8.

If you feel extravagant, it's nice to add chopped truffles or finely shaved baked ham to the soufflé. Also, you may serve it with a sauce that slightly resembles gazpacho: peel, seed, and chop tomatoes, a small amount of celery, and fresh basil. Mix with a small quantity of mild French dressing, using olive oil for one third of the oil portion.

Green Grape Sorbet

Wash enough Thompson seedless grapes to make 1 quart juice and blend them in an electric blender as fast as possible to eliminate the risk of their turning dark.

Strain the juice through a fine sieve, then add 1 cup of sugar per quart of juice, and a squeeze of lemon. Taste and add more sugar if needed. Use an electric sorbetier or pour into ice cube trays. If you use trays, remove from the freezer when the sorbet is partially frozen, whip, then return to the freezer.

Light Lunch with Blockbuster Desserts

FROM NANCY (MRS. ROBERT H.) DEDMAN

Nancy has always been interested in cooking, and has received certificates from the finest cooking schools in the world, including Cours de Cuisine at Maxim's in Paris, L'Ecole du Mougins in Mougins, and Robert Mondavi's Great Chefs course in New York City. She is also a full-time businesswoman and vice president and board member of her husband Robert's company, Club Corp International.

I first met Nancy several years ago when I gave a talk to the Dallas Women's Club. I had only just started lecturing, and I was nervous, but Nancy, my official greeter, put me right at ease.

Nancy admits that she loves rich, old-fashioned desserts; in fact, her dear friend Mrs. John Watson once gave her a birthday party where everything on the menu was made of chocolate. But Nancy, like most people, is trying to be more "heart healthy" these days. This luncheon is a perfect compromise.

"Nancy admits that she loves rich, old-fashioned desserts ...but, like most people, is trying to be more "heart healthy" these days."

M E N U

Cream of Butternut Squash Soup
with Cheese Toasts
Salad Mesclun with Grilled Chicken
and Threads of Vegetables
Sesame Dressing
Blue Corn Catfish Fingers with Pico de Gallo
Chayote Squash and Green Beans
Cornbread
Warm Baked Fudge with Cacao Ice Cream Sauce
garnished with Strawberries
* Orange Pudding

Orange Pudding

ORANGE PUDDING:

10 oranges, peeled and diced into bite-size chunks (do not section—cut crosswise in chunks)

1 cup sugar

CUSTARD FILLING:

1 quart milk

1 cup sugar

pinch of salt

5 heaping tablespoons flour

4 egg yolks, beaten

2 tablespoons butter

1 teaspoon vanilla

MERINGUE:

7 egg whites

pinch of salt

1/2 teaspoon cream of tartar

6 tablespoons sugar

To the peeled and diced oranges (including juice) add 1 cup of sugar and set aside.

CUSTARD FILLING:

Scald milk in the top of a double boiler over hot water. Mix together the second cup of sugar, pinch of salt, and flour. When milk is scalded, add the sugar-flour mixture to the milk, stirring constantly with a whisk until it is thickened slightly (about 10 to 15 minutes). Add a little of the hot mixture to 4 beaten egg yolks, stirring, then return it all to the thickened milk mixture on top of the double boiler. Cook again until thickened, stirring constantly (about 10 to 15 minutes).

Remove top half of double boiler from heat and add butter and vanilla. Let cool completely. Place the orange pieces with dissolved sugar and juice in an ovenproof soufflé dish, approximately 8 1/2 inches wide and 4 1/2 inches tall. Pour custard over the oranges.

MERINGUE:

Preheat oven to 350 degrees.

Beat egg whites, salt, and cream of tartar until stiff but not dry. Beat in sugar gradually, a tablespoon at a time, and continue beating until sugar is well blended and meringue holds stiff peaks. Pile meringue high and in peaks on top of custard. Spread well to the edge. Bake for 20 minutes. Do not burn! Let cool, then refrigerate. Serve very cold with strips of orange peel on top for decoration. This can be made the day before. Serves 8.

Afternoon Tea

FROM DIANA (MRS. MICHAEL) NATHANSON

Diana's husband Michael is the new young head of production for Columbia Pictures. Diana is an active, high-energy woman who loves to cook. In fact, before she found out she was pregnant, she planned to open her own restaurant in Los Angeles. I have no doubt she'll do it someday.

Diana told me, "The most important element in entertaining to me is a casual yet elegant atmosphere. I create this by using only the best of everything—even when it's just close friends in their jeans.

"I think my 'magic touch' comes with my eye for detail. I do everything myself—from the cooking to the table settings and flowers. Sometimes this causes guests to gravitate toward the kitchen to see everything that's going on, but that's part of the fun.

"My favorite occasion is afternoon tea. I love the pomp and circumstance of the age-old tradition. I have collected tiered trays, tea pots, tea strainers, enameled spoons, and linens from all over the world, and love to put them together to create an eclectic, traditional-yet-new afternoon tea."

M E N U

TEA SANDWICHES AND SAVORIES:
Smoked Salmon Canapés
Victorian Cucumber Sandwiches
* Puff Pastry Palmiers with Prosciutto and Fontina
* Caviar on Buckwheat Blinis with Crème Fraîche
Smoked Turkey on Orange/Cranberry Muffin
with Watercress and Honey Mustard
Warm Currant Scones with Devonshire Cream
and Fresh Berry Preserves

DESSERTS:
Madeleines • Walnut Cups
Scotch Shortbread • Harvard Brownies
Sugar Pecan Crisps • Chocolate-covered Strawberries
Lemon Tartlets

Puff Pastry Palmiers
with Prosciutto and Fontina

1 package (17¼ ounces) frozen
    puff pastry
honey mustard
½ pound thinly sliced prosciutto
½ pound thinly sliced fontina
    cheese
1 egg, beaten

Preheat oven to 350 degrees.

Spread mustard evenly over thawed puff pastry. Cover with 1 layer of prosciutto, then fontina. Roll each long side until it meets the center. Turn over and slice into ¼-inch-thick slices. Lay slices flat on parchment paper and brush lightly with the beaten egg. Bake until golden brown, about 10 minutes.

These can be served warm or at room temperature. As a variation, they may also be made with pesto and Parmesan cheese. Makes 50 to 60.

Caviar on Buckwheat Blinis
with Crème Fraîche

1 package active dry yeast
1½ cups warm water
1½ cups all-purpose flour
1½ cups buckwheat flour
3 eggs, separated
4 tablespoons melted unsalted
    butter
pinch of salt
1 teaspoon sugar
1½ cups warm milk
vegetable oil
crème fraîche (see appendix, p.188)
caviar
sieved egg yolk or finely chopped
    chives, for garnish

Soak yeast in water for 15 to 20 minutes. Slowly add all-purpose flour to yeast and let stand for 1 hour. Combine buckwheat flour, egg yolks, butter, salt, sugar, and milk with dough. Stir well to blend ingredients. Cover and let rise for 1 hour.

Just before cooking, beat egg whites until stiff and fold them into the mixture. Heat a heavy skillet until hot. Brush with vegetable oil and cook blinis in pancake fashion, using 1 tablespoon of batter for each, until golden brown.

To assemble, place a drop of crème fraîche on a cooled blini and then add caviar. Garnish with sieved egg yolk or finely chopped chives.

If you do not have time to make blinis, toasted white bread that has been cut into rounds with a cookie cutter and topped with caviar is equally nice. Makes 75 cocktail size.

Friday Buffet Supper
FROM PATRICIA KLUGE

Pat Kluge built a beautiful English country house in Virginia and when she was married to John, they used to host wonderful weekends with lots of friends. The following cold buffet was set out for guests as they arrived on Friday evening.

MENU

Hot Consommé Royale
served with Melba Toast
* Poached Eggs in Aspic
with Tomato Mayonnaise
Fillet of Beef in Madeira Aspic
Cold Roasted Quail with Wild Rice Salad
Whole Poached Salmon with Homemade Mayonnaise
Chicken Chaudfroid
Pâté de Foie Gras with Truffles
Hearts of Palm with French Olives & Thyme Vinaigrette
Tomatoes with Avocado Vinaigrette
Asparagus Vinaigrette
Belgian Endive Salad with Walnut Vinaigrette
Assorted Homemade Breads
Homemade Sorbets of Strawberry and Orange,
Kiwi and Calvados, and Mango and Apricot Brandy
Homemade Lace Cookies

Poached Eggs in Aspic with Tomato Mayonnaise

Carefully poach eggs to your liking. For each egg, add 1 drop of red wine vinegar to taste. Gently remove from water, trim excessive egg white, and let cool.

Place eggs in individual gelée molds, and cover with clear golden aspic (homemade or commercial). Allow to set for several hours, then remove from molds by dipping them into a bowl of warm water.

The Tomato Mayonnaise is made from homemade or commercial mayonnaise to which you add tomato purée (peeled, seeded, and chopped fresh tomatoes). Serve with homemade melba toast.

Sunday Night Supper Buffet

FROM NAN (MRS. THOMAS) KEMPNER

*N*an is a true New York mover and shaker—she seems to be everywhere. She sets the best table in New York, and always looks stunning. Nan will be the first to admit that, besides being a great cook, she's a real clotheshorse.

M E N U

* Bolliti Misti
Platter of Prosciutto and Avocado Slices
Platter of Sliced Tomatoes with Mozzarella and Basil
Cruets of Oil and Vinegar
Mixed Green Salad
Cheese Platter
Assorted Breads
Fresh Fruit Tarts

Bolliti Misti

Let sausage stand in cold water for 2 hours. Drain, prick all over with a fork, and wrap tightly in cheesecloth. Place in a kettle with quartered onion and celery, cover with water, and bring to a boil. Reduce heat and simmer for 1 hour. Remove from heat, but keep warm.

STUFFING CHICKEN:

Melt butter in medium fry pan. Sauté chopped onion and garlic until golden, add livers, and sauté 2 to 3 minutes. Remove to medium-sized bowl and add beaten eggs, soaked bread, prosciutto, parsley, Parmesan, black pepper, nutmeg, and salt to taste. Mix well and stuff chicken with the mixture. Sew up all the openings. Wrap it in several layers of cheesecloth, tie tightly, and refrigerate.

MEATS:

Parboil salt pork for 15 minutes, then drain. Place it in a kettle with beef, veal, and calf's foot, and cover with water. Boil

BOLLITI MISTI:

1 cotechino or zampone
   (2 pounds), or other spicy
   Italian sausage
3 medium yellow onions: 1
   chopped, 1 quartered,
   1 studded with cloves
2 ribs celery
2 tablespoons butter, or as
   needed
1 teaspoon minced garlic
3 good-sized chicken livers,
   chopped
3 eggs, lightly beaten
8 slices white bread, crusts
   removed, soaked in 1 cup milk,
   squeezed and mashed
10 ounces prosciutto, coarsely
   chopped
parsley, chopped including sprigs
2 cups grated Parmesan cheese
1/4 teaspoon black pepper
1/4 teaspoon grated nutmeg
salt
1 chicken (3 pounds), boned
1/2 pound lean salt pork
1 eye of round beef (2 pounds),
   cut into large chunks
1 veal shank (2 pounds), cut into
   large chunks
1 calf's foot
1 quart rich chicken broth, hot
8 large potatoes, peeled
8 carrots, peeled
sprigs of parsley, for garnish

for about 5 minutes. Remove scum as it rises. When clean, add clove-studded onion and cook gently for 1 hour. As liquid reduces, add the hot chicken broth. After 1 hour, add the chicken, and continue cooking for 45 minutes.

Remove the veal and keep it warm. Add the partially cooked, still-wrapped sausages. Cook for 1 hour more, then remove the beef, keeping it warm, and add carrots and potatoes. Continue cooking for 30 minutes. If beef and veal get cool, return to broth while unwrapping chicken and sausage.

Arrange meats and sliced sausages with vegetables around the stuffed bird. Decorate with sprigs of parsley.

Serve with degreased broth in a pitcher on the side and Green Sauce, Tomato Sauce, and Mostarda di Cremona (hot pickled fruit).

GREEN SAUCE:

Mix anchovy, parsley, pickles, potato, garlic, onion, and salt and pepper to taste in a food processor. Add oil for a mayonnaise consistency, then lemon juice or vinegar to thin. Salt and pepper to taste.

TOMATO SAUCE:

Slowly sauté garlic and onion in oil until they are very soft—almost to a pulp. Add tomatoes and cook briefly, just until they break down and get soft. Remove from heat and season with salt and pepper.

GREEN SAUCE:

4 anchovy fillets

$1/2$ cup chopped parsley

6 gherkins

1 medium potato, boiled, peeled, mashed

$1/2$ teaspoon minced garlic

2 tablespoons yellow onion

olive oil

lemon juice or vinegar

salt and pepper

TOMATO SAUCE:

1 clove garlic, minced

$1/2$ onion, minced

4 tablespoons olive oil

4 cups peeled, seeded, and chopped ripe tomatoes

salt and pepper

Outdoor Lunch in the Bahamas

FROM JACQUILINE, COUNTESS DE RAVENEL

Jacquiline de Ravenel and her husband Jean Charles live in Paris and the Bahamas. Their Nassau house has a view of both the bay and ocean. Jacquie is a beautiful and fascinating woman, a grandmother and the mother of a little girl at the same time. When her youngest daughter Rebecca was born, we used to joke in the family that someday she would marry my son Robert's firstborn, James Alfred Bloomingdale. Last year our two families were together at a square dance party in Jackson Hole, Wyoming, and James, looking very grown up at nine years old, asked Rebecca to dance. But she absolutely refused. Jacquie apologized for her daughter, but James said cheerfully, "That's okay. I got fifty cents to ask her."

For a heavenly experience, there is nothing quite like relaxing with the de Ravenels at their Nassau home and enjoying her marvelous food.

M E N U

Spicy Conch Chowder
Turkey
Fresh Asparagus with Hollandaise Sauce
Basket of Raw Vegetables
Scrambled Eggs with Truffles
* Oeufs au Moniere
Grouper Fish Fingers with Tartar Sauce
Fresh Grapefruit Salad

CREPES:
2 eggs
$1/3$ cup flour
pinch of salt
$1/2$ cup milk
5 teaspoons butter, melted
3 tablespoons beer

MUSHROOM SAUCE:
$1/4$ pound mushrooms, chopped
1 teaspoons onions, chopped
butter for sautéing

18 to 20 eggs
scallion tops

CHORON SAUCE:
$1/4$ cup dry white wine
$1/4$ cup wine vinegar
6 white peppercorns
$1^1/2$ tablespoons chopped shallot
3 egg yolks
12 tablespoons ($1^1/2$ sticks) butter
1 tablespoon tomato paste

Oeufs au Moniere

These are thin pancakes (crepes) with an egg in the center of each. Whisk eggs, flour, salt, and pour in milk slowly. Whisk in butter and beer and let it rest for 3 hours.

Lightly oil one or more blini (crepe) pans. Heat pan and pour in a small amount of batter. Heat briefly on top of stove and turn until crepe is light brown on both sides. This makes 18 to 20 crepes.

Make a mushroom sauce. Sauté mushrooms and onions in butter until they are soft. Place pancake/crepe on a plate, and put a teaspoonful of mushroom sauce in the middle.

Poach each egg for 3 minutes, then wrap it in a pancake, pulling up on either side and tying it with a string made of scallion tops so it resembles a handkerchief. This is served with a hot choron sauce, a Béarnaise with tomato paste instead of tarragon.
CHORON SAUCE:

Put wine, vinegar, peppercorns, and chopped shallot into a small sauce pan. Boil gently until liquid has reduced to about one third. Cool. Combine egg yolks and cooled reduction and add tomato paste. Cut butter into small pieces and add slowly to the egg yolk mixture over low heat.

Casual Dinner

FROM NANCY (MRS. RONALD) REAGAN

Nancy has been my dear friend for many years, long before her political days. My husband Alfred was one of the early group of people to see Ronald Reagan's potential. I am always aware that because of the President's and Nancy's choice in life, my own life has been different. I have many reasons to be thankful to them.

Nancy will be the first to tell you she's not a cook. But she has quite a sense of style and knows what to look for and what she wants. These days, the Reagans live a relatively quiet life. After years of formal occasions, they most enjoy small, informal dinners at their house in Bel Air, California. They are warm and unpretentious people, and everyone loves to be invited.

M E N U

Red Pepper Soup
* Chicken Pie
* Chocolate Soufflé with Sauce

I saved this recipe from Nancy's Sacramento days, where she spent eight years as the wife of the governor of California. She was happy to have it back when they returned to private life.

Chicken Pie

Boil stewing hen with green pepper, onion, and celery until meat is tender—about 1 hour. Remove meat from the bones, cut into chunks, and set aside.

Cook boiling onions for 20 minutes. Set aside.

MAKE WHITE SAUCE:

Mix sauce ingredients and cook over medium heat until the mixture is thick. If it becomes too thick, add more chicken stock. Add chicken and onions to the mixture.

CONTINUED

1 large stewing hen or roaster
1 green bell pepper
1 onion
2 stalks celery
12 white boiling onions

WHITE SAUCE:
$1/4$ pound (1 stick) butter
8 tablespoons flour
2 cups chicken stock
1 cup heavy cream
1 tablespoon each salt, black
    pepper, and poultry seasoning
2 tablespoons fresh chives

PIE CRUST:

2 cups flour

12 tablespoons ($^3/_4$ cup)
    shortening

1 teaspoon salt

5 to 6 tablespoons ice water

MAKE PIE CRUST:

Sift salt and flour, then blend the mixture with shortening. Add ice water. Makes 2 crusts.

Preheat oven to 400 degrees.

Line the bottom of a 3-quart casserole with the crust. Add sauce with chicken, and boiling onions, and arrange crust on top. Brush with butter. Cook pie for 10 minutes. Reduce heat to 350 degrees and cook for 50 minutes.

Chocolate Soufflé

6 tablespoons butter

3 squares semisweet chocolate

4 squares unsweetened
    chocolate

8 tablespoons flour

2 cups milk

5 egg yolks

1 cup sugar

$^1/_2$ teaspoon vanilla

$^1/_4$ teaspoon salt

6 egg whites

Preheat oven to 400 degrees.

Melt butter and chocolate in the top of a double boiler. Add flour. Add milk gradually. Stir constantly until the mixture is thick. Cool. Beat egg yolks and sugar until mixture is smooth and creamy. Add vanilla and salt to egg whites and beat until stiff. Add chocolate mixture to egg yolks and fold in egg whites. Place in 9-inch soufflé dish. Bake for 10 minutes. Reduce to 375 degrees and bake for 35 to 45 minutes.

Serve with chocolate sauce and whipped cream. Serves 6.

Dinner in the Kitchen
FROM DREDE MELE

Drede is a dear friend who lives in Paris, where for the past few years she has been the director of public relations for designer Georgio Armani. She adores her work, and loves to entertain. Drede thinks nothing of coming home after a busy day and organizing a dinner for friends. Like Drede herself, the menus are always inspired and original. The Warm Foie Gras with Apples is a favorite recipe from Les Landes, her country home in France.

M E N U

* Warm Foie Gras with Apples
Poached Salmon with Dill
Steamed Vegetables
Salad of Iced Mandarins
Wine: Red Bordeaux

Warm Foie Gras with Apples

Slice apples into thin pieces. In a frying pan, heat vegetable oil and margarine. Add apples and cook until they are soft and golden. Blot oil with a paper towel.

Add port wine and dash of freshly grated nutmeg.

Put apples aside and keep warm.

Add freshly ground pepper and a dash of salt to each of the 4 sides of the liver. Wrap the liver very tightly in aluminum foil so it is airtight. If there is more than 1 piece of liver, wrap separately.

Put a cast-iron skillet on top of the stove over a medium gas flame. Cook the foie gras in its aluminum foil case for 30 minutes. Every 8 minutes, turn it to another side. This should grill the meat, leaving no pink center.

When done, open the foil and drain the juice onto the bottom of the serving tray.

Cut the foie gras on the bias in diagonal slices

Place the sliced foie gras in the juice on the serving tray.

Squeeze the juice of fresh lemon on top.

Arrange apple slices around the foie gras and serve it warm. Serves 10.

4 medium apples
2 teaspoons vegetable oil
1 tablespoon margarine
2 tablespoons port wine
freshly grated nutmeg
freshly ground pepper and salt
$1\frac{1}{2}$ pounds foie gras of duck
$\frac{1}{2}$ lemon, juice only

Spring Dinner

FROM SUSAN (MRS. JOHN) GUTFREUND

My friend Susan lives in New York City and Paris, France. She's a marvelous hostess, and through the years she has always been very generous about sharing her recipes with me—which not every hostess will do.

"My idea of a perfect dinner party," Susan said charmingly, "is more than the graces but less than the muses. Whether there are eight guests or eighty, the most important factor is the attention to detail that seems to always make the difference between a good and a great evening.

"The greatest hostesses I've known leave nothing to chance. As I always say, anything that appears effortless is a lot of work! This attention, a good mix of guests, and the warmth of the hostess sets the tone for the evening."

Spring Dinner

M E N U

Salmon Cannelloni
* Deep-Fried Turkey
Leek and Potato Pie with Green Tomato Relish
Wicker Basket with Assorted Fruit
Sherbets in Individual Shells
Spice Cake

Deep-Fried Turkey

8-ounce bottle Italian dressing
4 tablespoons Worcestershire
    sauce
4 ounces ($1/2$ an 8-ounce jar) Dijon
    mustard
6 to 7 tablespoons Konricos or
    other Creole seasoning
10- to 12-pound fresh turkey (no
    larger than 12 pounds)
vegetable oil

Make a marinade with Italian dressing, Worcestershire sauce, mustard, and 4 to 5 tablespoons seasoning, and liquify it in a food processor.

Inject liquified marinade into the turkey breast and all through the turkey, using a syringe with a large-mouth needle. Sprinkle and rub 2 tablespoons of Creole seasoning all over the turkey.

Heat vegetable oil (enough to cover the entire turkey) to 350 degrees, checking temperature with a candy thermometer.

Deep-fry the turkey, 2 $1/2$ minutes per pound. The skin will turn quite dark.

Let stand at room temperature for 30 minutes, then slice thinly and serve.

Formal Dinner

FROM LEE (MRS. WALTER) ANNENBERG

For many years now, I have spent New Year's Eve with Lee and Walter at their Palm Desert estate. The Reagans also spend New Year's Eve with the Annenbergs, and did when they were in the White House. I must say, there's something special about welcoming in the New Year with the President of the United States, and dining beside my favorite Renoir hanging on the wall. Eventually, with the rest of the Annenbergs' collection, it will be hanging on a wall of the Metropolitan Museum, and I won't be dining beside it.

Lee is a fantastic hostess. Every detail is perfection. She and Walter are so gracious, and Walter can be very funny. At one dinner as the guests were oohing and aahing about the delicious food, and I was trying to get the recipe, he gave all the credit to Lee, saying, "I couldn't give you a recipe for water!"

The Annenbergs' favorite way of entertaining is to host a formal dinner.

M E N U

Sole/Salmon Mousseline
Lobster Sauce
Chicken Breast Cordon Bleu
Basket of Pommes Parisienne
Puree of Broccoli/String Beans
Glazed Carrots
* Strawberry Soufflé Glacé with Strawberry Sauce
Petits Fours

Strawberry Soufflé Glacé with Strawberry Sauce

Cook sugar to 250 degrees in 1 cup of water. Pour sugar mixture into egg whites while beating, and keep beating until well mixed. Transfer to a large bowl and let cool.

Add strawberry purée, strawberry extract, and lemon juice. Lastly, fold in the heavy whipped cream.

Fill soufflé dish that has been fitted with a waxed paper collar. Place in the freezer for at least 6 hours. Remove paper and decorate with fresh strawberries and grated chocolate. Serves 12.

STRAWBERRY SAUCE:

Blend all ingredients together in a blender. Strain and serve.

1^{1}/$_{2}$ pounds (3 cups) sugar
15 egg whites, beaten stiff
3^{1}/$_{2}$ cups strawberry purée, seedless, unsweetened
1^{1}/$_{2}$ tablespoons strawberry extract
^{1}/$_{2}$ lemon, juice only
3^{1}/$_{2}$ cups heavy cream, whipped

STRAWBERRY SAUCE:
1 pound fresh or frozen strawberries
^{1}/$_{2}$ pound (1 cup) sugar
^{1}/$_{2}$ lemon, juice only

Formal Dinner

FROM CARROLL (MRS. MILTON) PETRIE

Carroll, a dear friend of many years, lives in New York with her husband Milton. The Petries are known for being great philanthropists who take pleasure in helping people. If Milton reads a story in the paper that pulls at his heartstrings, he'll pick up the phone and make a call. Examples of their generosity include helping Marla Hanson, a young model whose face was slashed, and supporting the family of a New York policeman who was shot. The Petries are also involved in supporting the Metropolitan Museum, and are responsible for the beautiful Carroll and Milton Petrie Sculpture Court.

Carroll is admired as an international hostess who has entertained all over the world. She served this fabulous soufflé one night in New York, and everyone was wild about it. I was lucky to extricate the recipe from her, and I've prepared it several times. It's a real winner!

M E N U

Turban of Smoked Salmon and Smoked Trout Mousse
Tomato Sorbet
Melba Toast
Roast Stuffed Loin of Pork
with Apricots and Prunes
Whiskey Sauce
Purée of Yams with Marshmallows
Brussels Sprouts with Bacon, Scallions, and Walnuts
* Chocolate and Amaretto Soufflé
with Mocha Whipped Cream
Brownies

Chocolate and Amaretto Soufflé with Mocha Whipped Cream

MAKE THE CHOCOLATE MORSELS:

Melt the chocolate in a double boiler over low heat or in a microwave oven. Let cool until tepid.

On a cookie sheet lined with waxed paper, using a filled pastry bag with a very small (Number 0) tip, make small mounds of chocolate about the size of chocolate chip morsels. When all the chocolate has been used, put the cookie sheet in the freezer.

When the mounds are hard, remove them from the paper and put them in a bowl in the refrigerator.

Meanwhile, crumble the cookies (not too fine) and soak them in enough amaretto liqueur to cover.

MAKE THE CUSTARD:

Bring the milk to a boil in a saucepan. Put the egg yolks in a bowl, add the sugar, and beat immediately with a wire whisk for several minutes. Stir in the flour and beat until the mixture is very smooth. Pour on the boiling milk, whisking continuously.

Pour the custard back into the saucepan, set over medium heat and bring to a boil, stirring constantly. Cook for about 3 minutes and transfer the custard into a large mixing bowl. Cover with plastic wrap to avoid a skin forming.

ASSEMBLE THE SOUFFLE:

Preheat oven to 400 degrees.

Generously butter a 6-cup soufflé mold and dust with superfine sugar.

Beat the egg whites with a pinch of salt in an electric mixer until they form soft peaks. Then, using a wire whisk, quickly mix $1/3$ of the egg whites into the custard. With a spatula, fold in the rest, including the amaretto cookies and any liqueur not absorbed.

Pour $1/3$ of the soufflé mixture into the prepared mold and sprinkle the top with $1/2$ the chocolate morsels. Repeat the procedure. Finish with the last third of the soufflé mixture.

Bake for 30 to 35 minutes.

Dust the soufflé with confectioners' sugar. On the side, serve whipped cream flavored with coffee. Serves 6.

4 ounces bittersweet chocolate

1 scant cup Amaretti di Saronno cookies

amaretto liqueur

$1^1/2$ cup milk

6 egg yolks

$1/2$ cup sugar

$1/2$ cup flour

2 tablespoons soft butter

3 tablespoons superfine sugar

7 egg whites

salt

confectioners' sugar

whipped cream flavored with coffee

Formal Dinner in Rome

FROM BETTY (MRS. WILLIAM) WILSON

During the Reagan administration, Bill Wilson was able to establish diplomatic relations with the Vatican. Prior to that, the U.S.-Vatican relationship had been informal. In Rome, it was Betty and Bill's joy to entertain friends and members of the clergy. One always had a great time. In fact, it became a regular "pit stop" for their friends traveling in Europe.

This dinner was served at the Embassy, and luckily is still repeated at home in California. There's nothing like this recipe, which is quite complex to make, but well worth the effort. The serving dish is made of pastry, lid and all, and is filled with homemade pasta and sauce. You can make your own pasta, or use prepared.

M E N U

PASTA:
* Timballo di Mezzelune

MEAT:
Roast Loin of Veal

VEGETABLES:
Asparagus
Baby Carrots
Glazed Pearl Onions
Green Beans
Spinach

DESSERT:
Monte Bianco

Timballo di Mezzelune

Melt the butter in a small bowl, using a double boiler. Let the butter cool for $1/2$ hour. Make a mound of the flour on a pasta board and form a well in the center. Pour the melted butter into the well and then add the egg yolks, water, oil, sugar, salt, and nutmeg to the well. Use a fork to mix all the ingredients in the well together, then start incorporating the flour from the inside rim of the well until only 1 cup of the flour remains unincorporated.

Use your hands to gather the dough together, then knead it for 2 minutes and form it into a ball. Put the ball of dough in a floured cotton dish towel and let it rest in a cool place for 2 hours.

Unwrap the dough and knead it for 2 minutes on a pastry board. Sprinkle the board with the remaining flour, then cut the dough into 3 equal pieces. Using a rolling pin, roll out 1 piece to a thickness of a little less than $1/4$ inch. Make the lid of the timballo by placing the removable bottom of a 10-inch springform pan on the sheet of dough and cutting around it with a scalloped pastry wheel.

Preheat oven to 375 degrees.

Butter a baking sheet and place the timballo lid on it. Use a fork to make punctures all over the lid so the dough does not rise while it is baking. Cut out a circle or a square of dough about 2 inches across and place it in the center of the timballo lid to make a little handle.

To glaze, beat the egg in a small bowl and use a pastry brush to spread it over the top of the lid. Bake the lid for 35 minutes or until the pastry is golden brown.

While the lid is baking, roll out a second piece of the dough to the same thickness as the first. Cut a circular bottom for the timballo by placing the removable bottom of the springform pan on the pastry and cutting a circle $1/2$ inch larger than the bottom of the pan. Put the springform pan together and butter it. Fit the bottom layer of the timballo into the springform, curling the $1/2$-inch overlap up along the sides of the pan.

Take the third piece of dough and roll it out into a strip long enough to circle the inside of the springform pan. This strip will form the sides of the timballo. Use the rolling pin to

CONTINUED

PASTRY DRUM:

12 tablespoons ($1^{1}/2$ sticks) unsalted butter

5 cups unbleached all-purpose flour

2 extra large egg yolks

I cup cold water

4 tablespoons olive oil

1 tablespoon sugar

pinch of salt

pinch of freshly grated nutmeg

1 extra large egg (for glaze)

TIMBALLO DI MEZZELUNE, continued

stretch the strip of dough to a width of 3½ inches. Fit the strip of dough inside the springform along the sides, fitting it inside the overlapping pastry from the timballo bottom.

Use the palm of your hand to press down the pastry hanging over the top edge of the pan. Then use a knife to cut around the top to remove extra pastry.

By the time the pastry form is ready for the oven, the lid should have finished baking.

Fit a piece of aluminum foil shiny side up loosely inside the timballo, then put in weights or dried beans to keep the pastry from rising as it bakes. Place the pan in the oven and bake for 1 hour. Remove it from the oven and lift out the aluminum foil with the weights. Leave the pastry in the pan.

PASTA:

4 cups unbleached all-purpose flour

5 extra large eggs

pinch of salt

1 cup heavy cream

4 tablespoons grated Parmesan cheese

PASTA:

To make pasta by hand or with a manual pasta machine, put the flour in a mound on a pasta board. Use a fork to make a well in the center and put the eggs and salt in the well. Mix the contents of the well with the fork and incorporate the flour from the inner rim of the well. Start kneading the dough by hand to get an elastic ball of dough, then finish kneading by hand or with the rollers of the pasta machine. Stretch the pasta to a thickness of less than $1/16$ inch or to the finest setting of the machine.

To shape the pasta, make 2 rows of dots of filling (recipe below) 1 inch from each side, using 1 teaspoon of filling for each dot. Fold each side of the pasta over to cover the filling and press down around the dots of filling. Cut out half-moons or semicircles by placing only half of a round 2-inch jagged pastry cutter on each area of stuffing; seal each piece.

Bring a large stockpot of cold water to a boil. Add salt to taste. Add the half-moon pasta and cook for 2 to 3 minutes, depending on the dryness of the pasta. Use a strainer-skimmer to transfer the cooked pasta to the casserole with the sauce. Add the heavy cream, Parmesan cheese, and the pasta sauce.

PASTA FILLING:

¼ pound (1 stick) unsalted butter

4 ounces boneless beef sirloin

2 cloves garlic, peeled but left whole

3 whole cloves

salt and freshly ground black pepper

½ cup warm beef broth

½ cup freshly grated Parmesan cheese

½ cup unseasoned bread crumbs

PASTA FILLING:

Melt the butter in a small, heavy saucepan over medium heat. Add the meat and sauté for 4 minutes. Then add the garlic, cloves, and salt and pepper to taste. Cover the pan and cook for 2 minutes. Add the broth, cover the pan again, and cook over low heat for 15 minutes longer. Discard the garlic and cloves. Grind the meat finely and return it to the pan with its juice. Mix very well. Place the pan over medium heat and mix again. Remove from the heat and transfer the contents to a crockery or glass bowl to cool completely—about 1 hour. Then add the Parmesan cheese and bread crumbs, and salt and pepper to taste. Mix all the ingredients well and cover the bowl, until needed.

PASTA SAUCE:

Coarsely grind prosciutto, pancetta, chicken breast, and beef together in a meat grinder. Remove the skin from the sausage and put the sausage in a bowl. Add the ground meat and mix together with a wooden spoon.

Finely chop the carrot, onion, celery, garlic, and parsley on a board. Heat 6 tablespoons butter and oil in a casserole, preferably terra cotta, on medium heat. When the butter is melted, add the meat and sauté for 2 minutes. Then add the chopped vegetables and sauté, stirring occasionally until the onion is translucent (about 15 minutes). Add the wine and let it evaporate very slowly, about 15 minutes.

Dissolve the tomato paste in the hot broth and add it to the casserole. Salt and pepper to taste and let it simmer covered for 1 1/2 hours, stirring occasionally.

Fill the timballo with sauce and pasta and distribute 4 tablespoons butter, cut into pieces, over the top. Place the lid on the timballo and bake for 15 minutes.

Remove from the oven and allow to cool for 2 minutes, then transfer the springform pan to a large platter. Open and remove the form. Serve immediately, lifting the lid and spooning out individual servings. Serves 8.

PASTA SAUCE:

4 ounce piece of prosciutto

2 ounce slice of pancetta (salty bacon)

1 whole chicken breast (1 pound), skinned and boned

1 pound piece of boneless beef sirloin

1 sweet Italian sausage, without fennel, or 3 ounces finely ground pork

1 large carrot, scraped

1 medium red onion, peeled

1 celery stalk

1 medium garlic clove

10 sprigs Italian parsley, leaves only

10 tablespoons (1 stick plus 2 tablespoons) unsalted butter, divided

1 tablespoon olive oil

1 cup dry red wine

2 tablespoons tomato paste

2 cups hot chicken broth

salt and freshly ground pepper

Jerry's Favorite Dinner

FROM LILY (MRS. EDMOND) SAFRA

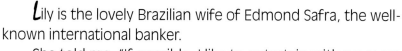

Lily is the lovely Brazilian wife of Edmond Safra, the well-known international banker.

She told me, "If possible, I like to entertain with no more than twenty-four guests, and I like to combine old friends and new acquaintances that I know will be at ease together.

"Setting the table is the part I enjoy most. Normally I decide first what I will use at the center of the table and the containers for the flowers, then the candleholders and according to them, the soup plates, then the porcelain, the crystal, and the cutlery. I like to mix different services according to the different courses. I pay a lot of attention to the table decor, using flowers, fruits, or even wild mushrooms.

"When I finish the center of the table, I always set one place by myself, then the butler does the others, following suit."

This dinner menu is the favorite of our mutual friend, Jerome Zipkin. In fact, Jerry once remarked, "If I were scheduled to go to the electric chair, this is the meal I would choose as my last."

M E N U

* Caviar in Aspic
* Lasagna Pie with Black Truffle Sauce
Endive Salad with Warm Goat Cheese
Pistachio Ice Cream with Hot Chocolate Sauce

Caviar in Aspic

ASPIC:
4 envelopes unflavored gelatin
8 cups consommé

ASPIC (GELEE):

Make a consommé (either regular or double consommé, see recipes below) and cool. Pour 2 cups of the cool consommé into a heavy 4- to 5-quart copper or enameled-iron saucepan and sprinkle the gelatin evenly over it. Soften for several minutes. Pour in the remaining 6 cups of consommé, set the pan over high heat and, stirring constantly, bring to a boil.

Pour it on 8 soup plates. Put in the refrigerator until it is hard. Then cut the centers with a mold 3 inches in diameter. Take the centers that you have cut off and fill them with caviar. Then put sour cream in a pastry bag and pipe it around the caviar. Serves 8.

TO MAKE THE CONSOMME:

Drop the celery leaves, leeks, carrots, parsley, tomatoes, egg whites, and egg shells in a heavy 4- to 5-quart copper or enameled-iron saucepan, mix well and pour in the stock. Set the pan over high heat and, stirring constantly, bring to a boil. Reduce the heat to low and simmer the stock uncovered for about 20 minutes. Do not stir. Then pour the contents of the pan slowly into a large sieve lined with a double thickness of dampened cheesecloth and set over a deep bowl. Allow the liquid to drain through without disturbing it.

TO MAKE DOUBLE CONSOMME:

For a richer double consommé, mix the raw meat with the basic vegetable ingredients. Use lean ground beef with beef stock, or chicken wings and backs with chicken stock. Pour in the stock and bring the mixture to a boil over high heat, stirring constantly.

Cook undisturbed and uncovered for 45 minutes then strain it following the directions above.

CONSOMME:

$1/2$ cup coarsely chopped fresh celery leaves

$1/2$ cup coarsely chopped green leek

$1/2$ cup coarsely chopped scraped carrots

$1/4$ cup coarsely chopped fresh parsley leaves and stems

2 medium-sized firm ripe tomatoes, coarsely chopped

$1/2$ cup egg whites

3 or 4 egg shells, finely crushed

2 quarts of beef or chicken stock, cold or cooled to room temperature

DOUBLE CONSOMME:

1 pound lean ground beef or 1 pound cut-up chicken wings and backs

Lasagna Pie with Black Truffle Sauce

LASAGNA:

Put the flour in a mound on the work surface. Make a well in the center and break the eggs into it. Add a pinch of salt and proceed to make the pasta dough. Roll out the dough into a thin sheet and cut into $3^1/2$-inch squares. Pick the leaves off the basil and purée them in a food processor with salt, garlic, pecorino, Parmesan cheese, olive oil, and pine nuts until creamy.

Drop the lasagna noodles into a pan of salted, boiling water and cook until they rise to the surface. Drain pasta, mix well with purée, and put into prebaked pie shell. Serve with truffle sauce (recipes on page 82). Serves 6 to 8.

CONTINUED

LASAGNA:

$10^1/2$ ounces ($2^1/2$ cups) all-purpose flour

3 eggs

salt

6 tiny basil plants, about 4 inches high

2 garlic cloves

1 teaspoon grated pecorino cheese

2 tablespoons Parmesan cheese

$1/2$ cup extra virgin olive oil

1 tablespoon pine nuts

LASAGNA PIE, continued

TRUFFLE SAUCE:
¹/₄ cup heavy cream
3 black truffles, with juice

PIE SHELL:
7 ounces (1³/₄ cups) all-purpose
    flour
1 teaspoon salt
3¹/₂ ounces (7 tablespoons)
    butter
1 dessert spoon water
1 egg yolk

TRUFFLE SAUCE:
    Boil cream until it becomes very thick. Add truffle juice and truffles, cut into julienne.

PIE SHELL:
    Preheat oven to 350 degrees. Measure flour and salt into bowl. Cut butter into flour with two knives or pastry cutter until it resembles cornmeal. Mix water and egg yolk. Add to flour and mix, adding more water if necessary, until ball forms. Chill for 30 minutes. Roll out to fit a deep 9-inch pie pan. Bake for 15 to 20 minutes.

Southern Dinner

FROM JANE (MRS. GUILFORD) DUDLEY, JR.

*J*ane's husband Guilford was ambassador to Denmark during the Nixon administration, and she has had great experience entertaining.

"In creating a really terrific dinner party, everything matters. There should be soft music and gentle candlelight. Your home should be slightly scented and filled with masses of open flowers, fresh from the garden.

"Try planning your dinners in different settings in and around your home: on a terrace, in a wine cellar, by the swimming pool, or simply in the garden under a gnarled tree. Occasionally we have a dinner party in our Nashville kitchen—which is brick and copper and wood—on an old English table which seats twelve. We did this on Halloween and had great fun arranging it. Two jack-o'-lanterns, facing in opposite directions, ruled the table. Thick candles in heavy brass candlesticks provided a soft glow. Twelve different small vegetables each held a place card and a small flower.

"But even with the perfect setting and perfect food, who sits on the chairs is more important than what is on the table. If possible, I always try to include someone unexpected—the more intelligent, amusing, glamorous, famous, the better! Even a couple from a different age group will add interest to your gathering.

"As for the menu, it's good to serve slightly unusual food, as long as your guests are likely to enjoy it. Presentation is almost as important as seasoning. Dishes can be presented on platters, in bowls, or in almost anything you like, but I believe no course should ever be served 'plated.'

"I am definitely not a minimalist. More is better—as long as the 'more' is marvelous."

M E N U

Sorrel Soup

Whole Wheat Biscuits

Baron D'L (Pouilly Fumé 1989)

Crabcakes

Cocktail and Tartar sauce

Oven-Baked New Potatoes in Skins

Thin Asparagus Tips Wrapped with Carrot Strips

Fresh Lima Beans

Grilled Tomato

French Rolls

Le Montrachet 1986

Salad:

baby arugula, perella, mâche, catalogna, autumn oak,

cocard, amaranth, lolla rosa, Belgian endive, baby spinach

Tomato-Basil Vinaigrette

Assorted Cheeses

Thin Toasted and Buttered French Melba

* Bombe aux Trois Chocolats

Homemade Vanilla Ice Cream

Fresh Raspberries

Veuve Clicquot La Grande Dame 1985

Coffee and Liqueurs

Bombe aux Trois Chocolats

MOUSSE:

12 ounces semisweet chocolate

1¹/₂ ounces (1¹/₂ squares)
    unsweetened chocolate

2¹/₂ teaspoons unflavored gelatin

3 tablespoons Jamaican rum

3 eggs plus 2 egg whites

1¹/₂ cups heavy cream

1¹/₂ tablespoons vanilla

3 tablespoons sugar

pinch of salt

FUDGE CAKE:

¹/₂ pound (2 sticks) unsalted
    butter

4 ounces (4 squares)
    unsweetened chocolate

2 cups sugar

3 eggs

1 teaspoon vanilla

¹/₂ teaspoon salt

1 cup flour

GLAZE:

4 ounces semisweet chocolate

¹/₂ ounce (¹/₂ square)
    unsweetened chocolate

MAKE MOUSSE:

Melt semisweet and unsweetened chocolate in the top of a double boiler.

Measure gelatin into a bowl and add rum. Let gelatin soften.

Separate eggs and reserve the whites. Beat the yolks with a whisk until thick.

Blend cream into the egg mixture and heat slowly over low heat, stirring with a wooden spoon, until the sauce coats the spoon.

Combine the gelatin and egg mixtures until the gelatin dissolves. Add melted chocolate, then vanilla.

Beat reserved egg whites plus 2 additional egg whites until they form stiff peaks. Add sugar and a pinch of salt, then beat until stiff peaks form. Fold egg whites into the chocolate and chill.

MAKE THE FUDGE CAKE:

Preheat oven to 350 degrees.

Melt 1 stick butter and the unsweetened chocolate in a double boiler.

Cream the remaining stick of butter with the sugar until fluffy. Beat in eggs, one at a time, then vanilla and salt.

Combine the egg mixture with the chocolate mixture. Fold in flour. Pour the batter into a 11 x 17-inch jelly roll pan, lined with wax paper. Bake for 25 minutes.

ASSEMBLE:

Cut a wax paper pattern of a bombe mold and place the pattern on the fudge cake sheet. Cut the fudge cake according to the pattern.

Line the mold with plastic wrap and arrange fudge cake in the mold. Fill with chocolate mousse. Top with fudge cake. Chill for 6 hours or overnight.

When ready to serve, loosen the bombe by pulling up on the plastic wrap. Unmold onto serving platter. Make the glaze by melting semisweet chocolate and unsweetened chocolate in the top of a double boiler. Pour it over the bombe, letting it drip down the sides. Serves 10 to 12.

See Egg Caution note in the appendix, page 188.

Spring Dinner for Margaret Thatcher

FROM CAROL (MRS. CHARLES) PRICE

This dinner was held at Winfield House, our U.S. Embassy residence in London, when Charles Price, with his beautiful wife Carol, was U.S. Ambassador to Great Britain. I was lucky enough to attend, and found Margaret Thatcher delightful and not at all formal.

MENU

Melon Squares Drizzled in Lime Juice with Prosciutto
Miniature Tart Shells with Creamy Artichoke Filling
Toast Rounds with Cream Cheese, Chives, Caviar
* White Gazpacho with Vegetable Garnish
Filets de Volaille Vauban
served with White Wine Sauce and Morels
Asparagus Bundles with Lemon Butter
Three Layer Timbales: Carrots, Broccoli, Cauliflower
Chocolate Mousse Cake with Raspberry Sauce

White Gazpacho
with Decorative Vegetable Garnish

Sauté onions and leeks in butter until translucent. Purée 1 cup of broth with cucumbers, garlic, and onion/leek mixture until smooth. Add flour and blend well. Combine sour cream, vinegar, horseradish to taste, Tabasco, white pepper, and salt in medium container and stir thoroughly. Allow to chill at least 6 hours.

Garnish with sorrel or opal basil leaves, cherry tomatoes, small julienned carrots, and asparagus tips. Serves 4 to 6.

GAZPACHO:
3 tablespoons unsalted butter
2/3 cup chopped onion
1 to 3 chopped leeks, white part only
3 to 4 cups hot chicken broth, divided
3 to 4 medium cucumbers, peeled, seeded, sliced thin
1 clove garlic
1 to 2 tablespoons flour
2 cups sour cream
3 tablespoons white wine vinegar
2 to 4 tablespoons creamy horseradish
1 teaspoon Tabasco
1 to 2 teaspoons white pepper
2 to 4 teaspoons salt
sorrel or opal basil leaves, cherry tomatoes, small julienned carrots, and asparagus tips for garnish

Staging Great Events

GIVING PARTIES WITH STYLE AND FLAIR

Every social occasion is an "event," but sometimes the setting, theme, or other aspect of a party is so special it stands out among the rest. I decided to devote a chapter to a collection of these outstanding events because, although you can't duplicate every detail of a dinner at the White House, or a Kentucky Derby spread, or a Spanish country picnic, you can take something from each to add a conversation-setting extra to your own parties. That might be serving a dish created for the Prince and Princess of Wales, or copying Joan Rivers's Christmas tea. It's a way for everyone to add a bit of glamour to life.

The events in this chapter were selected for their originality, style, and wonderful menus. To be sure, people today don't have extravagant parties like they once did, such as the Oriental Ball I attended in Paris, hosted by Baron Alexis de Rede, that included elephants lining the courtyard as we entered. Or the grand opening of the decorative arts wing of the Louvre Museum. Even the charity balls have toned down their extravagance. The truth is, you can create an outstanding party without spending a fortune, simply by borrowing the best from others.

What follows is a selection of events, followed by the kind of occasions everyone can relate to—those created around holidays.

SPECIAL EVENTS:

White House Dinner

Spanish Partridge Picnic Luncheon

Southern Gospel Supper

Kentucky Derby at Cave Hill House

Oscar Night at Spago

Election Night Tex-Mex

EVENTS TO CELEBRATE THE HOLIDAYS:

My Fourth of July Party

Bloomingdale Family Thanksgiving

Davis Christmas Party

English Christmas Tea

New Year's Eve in Palm Beach

PRESIDENT AND MRS. RONALD REAGAN

White House Dinner

FOR PRINCESS DIANA AND PRINCE CHARLES

I was fortunate to attend this wonderful party, given by President and Mrs. Reagan at the White House on November 9, 1985.

There's a style and ceremony to a White House occasion that simply cannot be matched. And Nancy Reagan always had such a clear idea of what she wanted to accomplish. She would take great care with every detail, from flowers to food.

I arrived the afternoon of the party, and was shown to the Queen's Room, where I would be staying—right across the hall from Lincoln's Bedroom. These rooms have an awesome sense of history, as you can well imagine. You can't help thinking about who else has slept in your bed!

Before dinner, I went downstairs to see all the beauty that was being created for the evening. Geranium trees had been placed on either side of the front door, and the entrance hall was banked with pyramid-shaped arrangements of pinkish-red geraniums. The East Room was decorated like an outdoor garden, with hedges and statues. The State Dining Room was beautifully set for dinner. There would be eighty guests, eight to a table. On each table were salmon-colored roses and four single silver candlesticks.

Before dinner, the Reagans received guests upstairs in their private quarters—something new for a dinner of this size. As I entered the room, my eyes were immediately drawn to Princess Diana, who was striking. She is very tall and was wearing an off-the-shoulder gown of midnight blue velvet. It was formfitting to mid-calf, then flared out so that when she danced, she looked like a mermaid.

We mingled for awhile, and were served delicious hors d'oeuvres—my favorite was the caviar in tiny cream puffs. I was at the table with Charles Price, our ambassador to the Court of St. James. My other tablemates included Estée Lauder, Tom Selleck, and John Travolta.

During dinner, John Travolta told me nervously that he was supposed to ask the Princess to dance later in the evening. "How should I hold her?" he asked. "Close? Distant?" I laughed. "Don't worry, John, you'll know when you get her in your arms."

The dancing took place after Leontyne Price sang, in the entrance hallway where cafe tables had been set up. Everyone watched Princess Diana and John Travolta on the dance floor. They were a spectacular couple!

My favorite course at dinner was the Lobster Mousseline, which Chef Henry Haller has graciously given me to use in this book. Nancy has always praised Mr. Haller highly. She says, "We tested and re-tested every recipe, and had 'tasting' dinners before each state dinner. Due to his boundless patience, the result was always exactly what I wanted."

"There's a style and ceremony to a White House occasion that simply cannot be matched."

Lobster Mousseline

2 fresh lobsters (2 pounds each)
4 tablespoons olive oil
$^1/_2$ cup finely minced shallots
2 garlic cloves, finely minced
1 cup chopped leeks, white part
    only
1 tablespoon salt
$^1/_8$ teaspoon black pepper
2 teaspoons fennel seed
$^1/_2$ cup warm brandy
1 cup homemade or commercial
    tomato sauce
1 tablespoon sweet paprika
$^1/_4$ teaspoon cayenne pepper
1 cup heavy cream, hot
2 packages ($^1/_4$ ounce each)
    unflavored gelatin
4 tablespoons dry sherry
2 cups heavy cream
10 thin slices black truffle or black
    olive
10 thin strips red bell pepper
10 fresh parsley sprigs
10 thin slices lemon
creamy horseradish sauce
herbed French bread

Remove the stomach and crack the claws of each lobster.

In a large pan, heat oil over medium high heat. Add whole lobsters and sauté until shells turn red. Add shallots, garlic, leeks, salt, pepper, and fennel seed. Sauté for 7 to 8 minutes.

Pour in warm brandy and flame carefully, using a long match. Let flames die out. Cover and simmer over medium heat for 5 minutes.

Stir in tomato sauce, paprika, cayenne pepper, and 1 cup hot cream. Cover and simmer 5 minutes more.

Transfer lobsters to a casserole dish and refrigerate to make removal of meat from shell easier.

Reduce the lobster broth over medium high heat to about 1 cup. Remove from heat and pour into a food processor.

Remove lobster meat from shells, chop fine, and add to food processor. Purée meat with broth for 3 minutes or until very smooth.

In the top of a double boiler, dissolve gelatin in sherry. Add the lobster purée and blend for 10 seconds. Transfer the mixture to a large mixing bowl.

In a clean, cold bowl, whip the 2 cups of cream until stiff, then fold into lobster mixture. Pour into a $1^1/_2$-quart ring mold, filling to $^1/_2$ inch from the top. Smooth the surface.

Refrigerate several hours or overnight.

Immerse mold briefly in hot water, then turn out onto a serving platter. Decorate the top with alternating truffle (or olive) slices and red pepper strips. Garnish the platter with alternating fresh parsley sprigs and lemon slices. Serve at once with creamy horseradish sauce (see below) and slices of herbed French bread. Serves 10.

HORSERADISH SAUCE:
1 cup sour cream
$^1/_2$ cup mayonnaise
$^1/_2$ cup freshly grated horseradish
    (or well-drained commercial
    horseradish)
pinch of salt
1 teaspoon Worcestershire sauce

CREAMY HORSERADISH SAUCE:
    Combine sauce ingredients and blend well.

Spanish Partridge Picnic Luncheon

ALINE, COUNTESS OF ROMANONES

Aline has been my friend for many years. In fact, it was she, an author and lecturer herself (*The Spy Wore Red*, and others), who encouraged me to write this book.

As a young woman in the OSS, Aline married the dashing grandee, Luis, and moved to his home in Spain. She quickly learned to love the culture and people and became a true Spaniard. Although she now spends a great deal of her time in New York, writing, her menus reflect the Spanish style.

Aline told me that her mother was a wonderful cook, but that she never was. "My husband always deplored that he had married the only American woman who did not know how to cook anything," she laughed. "For forty years, my mother sent me letters to Spain filled with recipes I never read. But although it's indisputable that I never had a penchant for cooking, I most certainly did for entertaining."

Aline has often told me about the luncheons she has served for years at her *finca* (ranch), Pascalete, in southwestern Spain. She makes a weekend event of it, sometimes hiring local people to entertain in costumes of the province—including gypsies who perform exotic flamencos in the evenings.

As Aline describes it, "After several hours of hiking in the rolling fields of live oak trees in Extremadura, which the province is called, guests usually have healthy appetites, which makes luncheon appreciated. I pick a spot where the open fire with the huge round cooking pan for the paella becomes the center of attention. Our tables are set up around that, and the bustle of cooks and the smell of food creates a picturesque scene which is fun to watch. In fact, seeing the food prepared on an open fire makes the luncheon a success before anyone even tastes it.

"In the country, people expect a feast, not a two-course meal. So our main dish of paella will be accompanied with a variety of homemade sausages, jamon serrano (Spanish smoked ham), and fabada (white beans with blood sausage cooked in a deep earthenware pot). We always have goat and sheep cheese, which is made on the property. Our paella is made with partridge and added shellfish, but chicken can be substituted."

Spanish Partridge Picnic Luncheon

M E N U

Homemade Sausages
Spanish Smoked Ham
* Partridge Paella
* Fabada
Goat and Sheep Cheese

Partridge Paella

¹/₂ cup olive oil, divided

1 medium onion, chopped

2 tomatoes, diced

¹/₂ pound mussels

¹/₂ pound shrimp

1 green bell pepper

1 medium squid

¹/₂ pound fish of choice

2 cups rice

salt

4 cups fish broth or water

several strips saffron

parsley

1 cup peas

1 red bell pepper, cut in strips

¹/₂ sliced red sausage, skin removed

1 partridge (cooked separately in a pressure cooker)

Place half of the olive oil in a frying pan to heat, add onion for 5 minutes, then tomatoes for another 5 minutes. Mash and pass through a sieve and pour into a round paella pan.

In a separate pot on the stove, place the mussels with some water. When the shells begin to open, remove pot from flame. Remove the shell halves that do not contain a mussel, reserving the other half. Cook shrimp until pink in same water and remove shells. Keep the broth to use later.

In the large paella pan where the rice will be cooked and later served, put the rest of the oil with the onion/tomato mixture. Cut the green pepper into small, square pieces and add. Add the squid, cut into long, wide strips. Cut the fish into small pieces and add. Finally, add the rice. Turn everything with a wooden spoon.

Add salt, then the broth of the mussels and shrimp. Add the 4 cups of fish broth until the mixture is covered. Move the pan, shaking it so the water and broth will cover the rice. Do this on a medium fire.

Meanwhile, in another container, mash the saffron and the parsley with a bit of salt and a couple tablespoons of warm water and pour over the rice. Move the pan again to cover everything. Now place the shrimp on top of the rice, evenly and attractively distributed. Add peas when the broth is half consumed, place the strips of red pepper, mussels and sausage on top, plus strips of partridge.

Cook about 20 minutes or until the rice is tender. Remove from the fire and let stand about 5 minutes.

Some people like paella with a golden crusty bottom. This is more easily accomplished when the paella is cooked on an open fire. The underneath crust is added to each serving by scraping a bit from the bottom of the pan. The rice should be slightly yellow from the saffron. Serves 8.

Fabada

Soak beans for 3 hours in cold water. Place in deep pot and cover with cold water. Put on heat and when water begins to boil add more cold water—enough to stop the boiling. Repeat this process 3 times. In Spain, this is called "scaring the beans." It's what makes them tender. Once the beans are "scared" enough, and with just enough water to cover them, add ham, bacon, veal knuckle, oxtail, olive oil, garlic, and red pepper.

Cook the fabada on medium heat for $2^1/_2$ to 3 hours. Add the blood sausage $^1/_2$ hour before finishing. Add a dash of salt at the last minute. Serves 20.

$2^1/_2$ pounds large white beans (about $6^1/_4$ cups)
large piece of smoked ham
$^1/_2$ pound bacon
1 small veal knuckle
1 piece oxtail
$^1/_2$ cup olive oil
1 to 2 cloves garlic
1 tablespoon cayenne pepper
3 fresh blood sausages
salt

❧

Aline told me, "On some occasions, we host a dinner where we serve partridge. This is my favorite way to prepare it."

Partridge with Grapes

Wash partridges, salt, and grease inside and out with butter. Fill the insides with peeled grapes.

Heat olive oil in a saucepan, add the partridges, and brown them on all sides, turning them over carefully to avoid piercing them. Once golden, cover with wine and water and sprinkle with pepper. Cover the pan and cook for about 1 hour on low heat, turning them over now and then.

Peel more grapes. When partridges are tender, surround them with peeled grapes.

Heat cognac in a small pan, then light with a match and pour the flaming cognac over the partridges. Cover the pan and leave for another 5 minutes on medium heat.

Serve partridges sliced in half, lengthwise, surrounded by grapes and covered with sauce. Serves 6.

3 partridges, small and tender
salt and pepper
3 tablespoons butter
1 pound white grapes
3 tablespoons olive oil
1 cup white wine
3 tablespoons cognac

Southern Gospel Supper

CONNIE AND W. RANDALL JONES

This was a terrific party I attended in New York, hosted by Connie and Randall Jones. He is the publisher of *Worth* magazine. I met the Joneses when they were visiting California, and was charmed by their warmth and style—which is all-Southern. Randall Jones, who was born and raised in Atlanta, loves to incorporate old family recipes in events he creates for the magazine. The food for this Southern Gospel Supper was wonderful, and the mood of the occasion was uplifting and fun. Throughout the evening, a glorious gospel choir from Harlem entertained.

M E N U

Vidalia Onion, Gruyère, Bacon Squares
Sweet Bacon
Spicy Sausage Pinwheels
Fried Chicken
Chicken Fried Steak and Gravy
Corn on the Cob
Sweet Potato Soufflé
Fried Okra
Collard Greens
* Buttermilk Biscuits
Buttermilk Cornbread
Pecan Pie
Fudge Cake
* 'Malgamation Cake

Buttermilk Biscuits

2 cups self-rising flour, sifted
1/3 cup shortening
3/4 cup plus 1 tablespoon
 buttermilk

Preheat oven to 450 degrees.

Combine flour and shortening in a medium-size bowl. Cut in shortening until the mixture resembles coarse meal. Stir in buttermilk with a fork. Turn dough onto a floured surface and knead lightly 3 to 4 times. Roll dough to 1/2-inch thickness and cut into bite-size biscuits with a miniature biscuit cutter. Place biscuits on an ungreased baking sheet and bake for 8 to 10 minutes. When ready to serve, slice in half and stuff with small pieces of country ham and add spicy mustard. Or just eat them plain with butter and jam. Makes 24.

৵

Randall told me the story of this cake recipe. "This is 'Southern short' for Amalgamation Cake, meaning a cake composed of an amalgamation of whatever can be found in the cupboard. It dates back to the Civil War, when the contents of people's cupboards were often unpredictable. Thus the ingredients often changed. My mother has made many modifications over the years. It's a Southerner's answer to the fruit cake, and is always around the house during the holidays. Mother sent a cake for the Gospel Supper and it seemed to be very well-received by 'Yankees.' It's even better when served with homemade wine."

'Malgamation Cake

Preheat oven to 325 degrees.

Grease and prepare three 9-inch cake pans with shortening and a light dusting of flour.

Cream together shortening and sugar until fluffy. Sift together salt, flour, and baking powder. Add slowly to creamed mixture, alternating with milk. Fold in egg whites and vanilla. Bake 20 to 25 minutes until it is lightly browned and the sides begin to pull away from the pans. Cool on wire racks. Dust off loose crumbs before frosting.

FILLING AND ICING:

Mix together egg yolks, sugar, and milk in a heavy saucepan. Stir constantly over medium high heat. Cook until thick. Add butter. Stir well to incorporate butter thoroughly. Remove from heat. Stir in nuts, raisins, and wine. Cool until thickened to spreading consistency.

Frost each layer and the sides with icing. Decorate with candied cherries and coconut. Keep refrigerated before serving. Serves 16 to 20.

CAKE:
1 cup shortening
2 cups sugar
pinch of salt
3 cups sifted flour
3 teaspoons baking powder
1 cup milk
6 egg whites, stiffly beaten
1 teaspoon vanilla

FILLING AND ICING:
6 egg yolks, well beaten
2 cups sugar
1 cup milk
$1/4$ pound (1 stick) unsalted butter
1 cup English walnuts or pecans
$1/2$ cup golden raisins, finely chopped
$1/4$ cup sweet red wine
garnish of candied red and green cherries
1 cup freshly grated coconut

Kentucky Derby at Cave Hill House

GOV. JOHN Y. BROWN, JR. AND PHYLLIS GEORGE BROWN

Phyllis is a talented and beautiful woman who has made her mark again and again—from being Miss America, to hosting CBS's "Morning Show," to being national spokeswoman for Save the Children. In 1979, she married John Brown, then governor of Kentucky, and she brought a special style and energy to her role as First Lady. Shortly after their marriage, the Browns purchased Cave Hill Place, a historic site built by a prominent early American settler. Phyllis set about restoring and redecorating and it has become a showplace for antiques and Kentucky crafts. Phyllis describes the result in her book, *Kentucky Crafts: Handmade and Heartfelt.*

Each year, on the Sunday night after the Kentucky Derby, Phyllis and John host a wonderful party. The servers are all dressed as Southern belles, and the house and grounds are filled with Kentucky crafts. The menu is mouth-watering. Of course, Phyllis, the creator of Chicken by George, is quite a cook.

Phyllis told me, "For me, the magic to entertaining is making everyone feel comfortable and at home. Also, it's important to pay close attention to details. The best compliment is when someone says, 'I've had such a wonderful time, I don't want to leave!'

"Kentucky Derby time is the perfect occasion for a party because it is the most lovely time of the year. The dogwoods are in bloom, and the bluegrass is glowing."

M E N U

* Mint Juleps
Pine Oak Asparagus
Cave Hill Corn Pudding
* Cheese Grits
Spoon Bread
Chicken by George
Country Western Dill
* Ambrosia
Beaten Biscuits • Country Ham
Kentucky Derby Pie
* Toffee Chocolate Mousse Pie
Fruit Platter

Mint Juleps

Combine sugar and water and bring to a boil. Let simmer for 10 minutes until thick and clear. While hot, stir in 1 bunch of mint sprigs. Let cool. Then strain the syrup into a small container. Discard the mint.

When ready to serve, pour 2 ounces ($^1/_4$ cup) of bourbon and 2 ounces ($^1/_4$ cup) of syrup into each ice-filled, frosted cup. Add a sprig of mint. Serves 12.

Cheese Grits

Preheat oven to 300 to 325 degrees.

Cook grits in boiling water. When thick, add butter and garlic cheese, then stir until both are melted.

Beat eggs lightly and stir into grits along with seasoning salt. Pour into an oblong buttered glass casserole. Bake for 1 hour. A sheet of aluminum foil placed under the pan will prevent the bottom from scorching. Serves 6 to 8.

Ambrosia

Drain all fruit. Cut strawberries in half. Cut pears and pineapples into bite-size pieces. Pit cherries. Mix together, then fold in sour and whipped cream. Serves 8 to 10.

MINT JULEPS:

3 cups sugar

1$^1/_2$ cups water

2 bunches fresh mint, divided

24 ounces (3 cups) Kentucky bourboncrushed ice

CHEESE GRITS:

1 cup quick-cooking (not instant) grits

4 cups boiling water

$^1/_4$ pound (1 stick) butter or margarine

2 links (6 ounces each) processed cheese with garlic

2 eggs

2 teaspoons seasoning salt, or more to taste

AMBROSIA:

2 cups fresh chunked pineapple

2 cups fresh strawberries

2 cups mandarin oranges

2 cups canned pear chunks

1 cup Royal Anne cherries

1 cup miniature marshmallows

2 cups sweetened coconut

1$^1/_2$ cups sour cream

1$^1/_2$ cups heavy cream, whipped

Toffee Chocolate Mousse Pie

CRUST:

1 pound (3^1/$_2$ cups) pecan pieces
^{1}/$_4$ pound (1 stick) unsalted butter
^{1}/$_2$ cup sugar
^{1}/$_4$ cup water

THE CRUST:

Preheat oven to 325 degrees.

Grind pecans in a food processor for about 45 seconds, then place in a mixing bowl.

Melt butter completely and add sugar. Keep beating and stirring over medium heat until thick, smooth paste (about 5 minutes). Remove from heat and add water, stirring constantly to create a syrup. Pour mixture over pecans and mix thoroughly.

Butter and flour two 12-inch tart pans. Press pecan mixture into pans and bake for 10 minutes or until golden brown. Remove and let cool at room temperature. Yields two 12-inch pie crusts.

MOUSSE:

28 ounces semisweet chocolate
^{1}/$_4$ cup vegetable oil
4 cups heavy cream

THE MOUSSE:

In a double boiler, melt chocolate and add vegetable oil. Chocolate should be smooth and almost liquid.

Whip cream to form soft peaks. Add hot chocolate while stirring constantly. When chocolate and cream are combined, refrigerate for 2 hours.

Remove from refrigerator and stir by hand, making sure mousse is smooth and without lumps. Spoon into pastry bag and pipe mousse into pecan crust. Refrigerate pies.

SAUCE:

1 pound (4 sticks) unsalted butter
3^1/$_2$ cups sugar
4 cups heavy cream

THE SAUCE:

Melt butter over medium high heat and add sugar. Stir mixture frequently. Continue this process until mixture has reached a deep caramel color. Butter and sugar will be separating at this point; no problem. Remove from heat and while stirring constantly, add heavy cream. Caution: When adding the cream, the mixture will bubble up and release very hot steam. Use a whisk with a long handle or wear an oven mitt to avoid getting burned. After cream is added, strain toffee sauce into a container and let it cool. Keep sauce refrigerated and heat right before serving. Yields 2 quarts.

To serve, cut each pie into 6 to 8 pieces. Ladle about ^{1}/$_4$ cup of sauce over each piece. Serves 12 to 16.

Oscar Night at Spago

MARY AND IRVING ("SWIFTY") LAZAR

Swifty, the famous and outstanding literary agent, was the mover and shaker of Hollywood. People would do just about anything for an invitation to his Oscar night party at the restaurant Spago. His party became nearly as famous as the Oscars themselves.

The invitation was always for 5:00 P.M. Swifty was very strict about this, since everyone had to be seated by 6:00, which is when the Oscars are televised in Los Angeles. We sat at long tables facing several TV screens, and during the three-plus hours, waiters passed miniature pizzas and other goodies. Dinner began after the show when people arrived in droves from the Academy Awards show itself. Win or lose, everyone was in a happy, social mood, and it was fun to share your table with the likes of Michael Douglas, Madonna, Michael Jackson, Warren Beatty, and many other stars. I must admit, sometimes it was hard not to gawk like a teenager in such celebrated company!

This is the menu for the Lazar Oscar Party held on March 31, 1992.

M E N U

Piper Heidsieck Cuvée Brut
Sanford Chardonnay, Santa Barbara 1990
Joseph Phelps "Insignia" Cabernet Sauvignon, Napa 1982
Eureka California Lager
San Pellegrino & Fonte Limpia Waters
New Potatoes with Two Caviars
* Smoked Salmon Pizza with Caviar
Chicken and Beef Satés
Smoked Seafood Springrolls
Chinese Duck Sandwiches
Sautéed Pacific Oysters with Spicy Salsa
Assorted Spago Pizzas
Chino Ranch Chopped Vegetable Salad
Oven Roasted Alaskan White Salmon with Potato Purée and
Cabernet Butter Sauce
Oscar's Favorite Desserts

Smoked Salmon Pizza with Caviar

PIZZA DOUGH:

3 cups all-purpose flour

1 teaspoon salt

1 tablespoon honey

2 tablespoons olive oil

$^3/_4$ cup cool water

1 package fresh or dry yeast

$^1/_4$ cup warm water

PIZZA DOUGH:

Place the flour in a food processor. Combine the salt, honey, olive oil, and the $^3/_4$ cup cool water in a small bowl or measuring cup. Mix well. Dissolve the yeast in the $^1/_4$ cup warm water and let proof for 10 minutes.

With the motor running, slowly pour the salt and honey liquid through the feed tube. Then pour in the dissolved yeast. Process until the dough forms a ball on the blade. If it is sticky, add sprinklings of flour. Transfer the dough to a lightly floured surface and knead until it is smooth. Place in a buttered bowl and allow the dough to rest, covered, for 30 minutes.

To make the dough in an electric mixer fitted with a dough hook, place the flour in the bowl and add the ingredients in the same order as when using a food processor. Knead the dough in the machine until it forms a smooth ball. Place the dough in a buttered bowl and allow it to rest, covered, for 30 minutes.

To prepare by hand, place the flour on a work surface and make a well in the center. Add the wet ingredients and proofed yeast. Slowly incorporate the flour into the wet ingredients, working from the center outward. When a dough forms, knead it on a floured surface until smooth. Place in a buttered bowl and allow the dough to rest, covered, for 30 minutes.

Divide the dough into 4 equal parts. Roll each piece into a smooth, tight ball. Place on a flat sheet or dish, cover with a damp towel, and refrigerate.

One hour before baking, remove the dough from the refrigerator and let it come to room temperature. Lightly flour a work surface. Using your fingertips, flatten each ball of dough into a circle, about 6 inches in diameter, making the outer edge thicker than the center. Turn the dough over and repeat. Lift the dough from the work surface and gently stretch the edges, working clockwise to form a 7- to 8-inch circle. Repeat with the other 3 pieces. Place the circles on a lightly floured wooden peel or on baking sheets.

You can also roll out the pizzas with a rolling pin, then pinch up the edges with your fingers to form a little ridge.

PIZZA TOPPING:

Preheat the oven, with a pizza stone inside, to 500 degrees for 30 minutes.

Cut the salmon into paper-thin slices. Reserve. Brush the center of each pizza to within 1 inch of the edge with olive oil and sprinkle it with some of the red onion. Slide the pizza onto the stone and bake it for 8 to 12 minutes, or until the crust is golden brown.

Mix the dill with the sour cream or crème fraîche and freshly ground pepper to taste. Transfer the pizzas to heated dinner plates and spread them with the sour cream mixture. Divide the salmon, and arrange it decoratively on top.

Place 1 tablespoon golden caviar in the center of each pizza, then spoon a little of the black caviar in the center of the golden caviar.

Garnish each pizza with a small dill sprig, and serve from the heated dinner plates. Makes four 7- to 8-inch pizzas.

PIZZA TOPPING:

3 to 4 ounces smoked salmon

$1/4$ cup extra virgin olive oil

$1/2$ medium red onion, cut into julienne strips

$1/4$ bunch fresh dill, minced, plus 4 small sprigs for garnish

$1/3$ cup sour cream or crème fraîche

freshly ground pepper

4 heaping tablespoons domestic golden caviar

1 heaping teaspoon black caviar

Election Night Tex-Mex

GEORGETTE AND ROBERT MOSBACHER

Georgette Mosbacher is a wonderful hostess with great imagination, in addition to being a very successful business-woman. During the late 1980s, while Robert served as Secretary of Commerce under George Bush, they entertained beautifully in their Georgetown house.

The Mosbachers have always been involved in politics and, not surprisingly, one of Georgette's most memorable parties was the one she gave on election night in 1988. "We were still spending most of our time in Texas," she recalls, "and we decided to give a party for our friends in New York. We had been on the campaign trail for George Bush and many of our friends rallied around us in our efforts for his election. We wanted to do something special—and something that was an appropriate reflection of ourselves and of George Bush. I found a Tex-Mex restaurant in New York called the Cadillac Bar and arranged to hold our party there. When I sent out the invitations, we didn't know if George Bush was going to win, so the invitations read:

Georgette and Robert Mosbacher
invite you to celebrate the election
(or drown our sorrows)
at a Tex-Mex dinner

"The invitations were rolled up and wrapped in a bandanna scarf. At the dinner, we had a sheriff's badge for each of the guests with the table number on the badge. We had shoe shiners to shine the guests' boots. We also had a man dressed up in cowboy attire who circulated the room taking instant pictures of each person.

"The table centerpieces were inverted straw cowboy hats with cactus plants. Pitchers of margaritas and beer, and bowls of chips and salsa, were on each table. 'Shooter girls' roamed the room offering shots of tequila.

"During cocktails we had a mariachi band, and during and after dinner there was a band that played country western and Top 40 songs."

The menu for the evening was purely Texan, served by the creative people at the Cadillac Bar. Everyone had a wonderful time, and the success of the party demonstrated that one can entertain in a restaurant, if everything is carefully organized ahead of time.

5 tablespoons olive oil

3 onions, thinly sliced

2 garlic cloves, chopped

2 green peppers, seeded and thinly sliced

3 medium-sized eggplants, seeded

3 medium zucchini in $1/2$-inch-thick slices

4 large tomatoes, skinned and chopped

salt and freshly ground pepper

$1/4$ teaspoon each fresh or dried rosemary, thyme, and basil

This is Georgette's favorite recipe for ratatouillee.

Ratatouille

Heat the oil over low heat in a heavy pan. Add the onions and garlic and cook for five minutes or until they are soft but not brown. Add peppers, eggplants, and zucchini, stir well and cook over very low heat for at least 30 minutes, stirring from time to time.

Add the tomatoes and season well with salt and black pepper. Add the herbs and cook for another 30 minutes on low heat. Serves 6 to 8.

EVENTS IN CELEBRATION OF THE HOLIDAYS

My Fourth of July Party

Almost every year, I give an outdoor party to celebrate the Fourth of July, inviting around fifty people. It's a festive occasion, and, as always, I work well ahead of the date. I do a little each day, starting with the guest list and invitations, then the menu, help, shopping list, music, parking, flowers, tables, and so on. I use my lovely Bicentennial china, and of course the color scheme is red, white, and blue.

This year, it was a very special occasion, since it doubled as a birthday party for Nancy Reagan and also for my friend Joe Hannan.

The buffet was plentiful—lots of heaping plates of hearty all-American food, with tables set in the atrium. A live band played John Philip Sousa marches before dinner and dance music after. Since people are usually a bit shy about starting to dance, I got the ball rolling, inviting Jimmy Stewart to have the first dance. Jimmy is still one of the best dancers I know.

The evening ended near midnight, and we all felt it had been a perfect way to express our friendship. One thank-you note, from Mrs. Sean Connery, read, "It was one of the most beautiful and romantic evenings I've spent." Notes like that make it worth the effort.

MENU

Knockwurst and Sauerkraut
* Chicken-Chive Burgers
Cold Filet of Beef
Medallions of Salmon
Cole Slaw
* Ham and Cheese Macaroni
Sliced Tomatoes with Basil
* Best Vanilla Ice Cream (recipe on page 53)
with Shaved Chocolate and Peppermint
* Chocolate Sauce (recipe on page 53)
Birthday Cake

Chicken-Chive Burgers

4 chicken breast halves, skinless
and boneless

1½ cups finely chopped bread
crumbs, divided

½ cup chicken broth, divided

¼ cup heavy cream

2 tablespoons finely grated onion

½ teaspoon ground cumin

salt

freshly ground pepper to taste

2 tablespoons vegetable oil

4 tablespoons butter, divided

2 tablespoons finely chopped
fresh chives

Cut chicken into 1-inch cubes and place them in a food processor. Blend thoroughly. Put the chicken in a mixing bowl and add ½ cup of bread crumbs, ¼ cup of chicken broth, and the cream, onion, cumin, and salt and pepper. Using your fingers, mix well.

Spoon the remaining cup of bread crumbs onto a flat surface. Divide the chicken mixture into 4 portions. Shape each portion into a ball and roll it in the bread crumbs. Then flatten each ball into a patty, about ³/₄-inch thick.

Heat oil in a nonstick skillet. Add the patties and cook over medium low heat for about 5 minutes or until they're nicely browned on one side. Turn patties and cook for another 5 minutes or until the reverse side is browned. Place cooked patties on a warm platter.

Heat 2 tablespoons of butter in a small saucepan and add the remaining ¼ cup broth. Bring to a boil, stirring with a wire whisk, and cook until the liquid is reduced by half. Gradually add the remaining 2 tablespoons of butter, stirring with a whisk. Stir in chives and pour the sauce over the burgers. Serves 4.

Ham and Cheese Macaroni

2 cups uncooked macaroni

salt

³/₄ pound thickly sliced cooked
ham

¼ pound mushrooms

½ pound sharp cheddar cheese

3 tablespoons butter, divided

1 tablespoon flour

2 cups milk

½ teaspoon freshly grated
nutmeg

freshly ground black pepper to
taste

½ cup finely chopped onions

⅛ teaspoon cayenne pepper

1 cup heavy cream

3 tablespoons freshly grated
Parmesan cheese

Preheat oven to 425 degrees.

Bring 3 quarts of water to a boil and add salt if desired for taste. Cook the macaroni until it is tender—about 10 to 12 minutes. Drain water and return macaroni to the pot.

Cut ham into ½-inch cubes and set aside.

Slice the mushrooms.

Cut the cheddar cheese into slices about ¼-inch thick. Stack the slices and cut them into ¼-inch wide strips. Then cut the strips into ¼-inch cubes.

Melt 2 tablespoons of butter in a saucepan and add the flour, stirring with a wire whisk. Cook for about 1 minute, then add the milk and stir briskly with a wire whisk. Let simmer for about 1 minute, then add the nutmeg, cheddar cheese, salt to taste, and black pepper.

Heat the remaining tablespoon of butter in a skillet and add the onions and mushrooms. Cook, stirring, until the mushrooms are wilted. Add the ham and cook, stirring, for 1 minute. Add the cheese sauce, cayenne, and cream. Cook, stirring, for another minute.

Pour and scrape the mixture into the macaroni and mix well. Transfer to a buttered 10-cup baking dish. Sprinkle the top with Parmesan cheese and place it in the oven. Bake for 10 minutes. Then turn the broiler up to high and brown the macaroni and cheese under the broiler until the top is nicely browned—about 2 to 3 minutes. Serves 6.

A Family Thanksgiving
THE BLOOMINGDALES

My favorite day of the year is Thanksgiving, when the entire family gathers together. There isn't the pressure of Christmas, so we can concentrate on making it warm and meaningful. Since I grew up as an only child, it is important for me to have everyone gathered. I adore the fact that I am the head of a large and happy brood, and there is no occasion when this is more apparent than Thanksgiving.

MENU

Mushroom Soup

* Turkey with Shallot Stuffing

Giblet Gravy

* Cranberry Relish

Green Vegetable

* Fran's Yam Pudding

* Bertie's Pecan Pie

"My favorite day of the year is Thanksgiving, when the entire family gathers together. There isn't the pressure of Christmas, so we can concentrate on making it warm and meaningful."

Turkey with Shallot Stuffing

SHALLOT STUFFING:

12 tablespoons (1½ sticks) butter
10 cups bread crumbs, from French or Italian bread
2 cups shallots, finely chopped
½ cup fresh parsley, chopped
1 tablespoon dried tarragon
2 teaspoons salt
1 teaspoon freshly ground pepper

TURKEY:

1 pound turkey, about 20 pounds
3 tablespoons vegetable oil
salt and pepper
2 onions, peeled
1 cup chicken broth
1 cup water

CRANBERRY RELISH:

1 large orange
1½ cups sugar
¾ cup water
¼ cup lemon juice
3 cups fresh cranberries

SHALLOT STUFFING:

In a saucepan, melt butter. Remove from the heat and stir in bread crumbs, shallots, and seasonings. Mix well.

TURKEY:

Stuff the turkey cavity with about 5 cups of Shallot Stuffing. Fill the neck opening with the remaining stuffing and fold over the skin. Truss the turkey with string.

Place the turkey in a large roasting pan, and rub it with oil, salt, and pepper. Place the onions around it. Roast for about 45 minutes at 450 degrees, then baste and cover the top loosely with aluminum foil.

Reduce heat to 400 degrees. Continue roasting for another 50 minutes, then pour chicken broth and water around the turkey. Replace foil and continue baking, basting every 15 to 20 minutes. Total cooking time is about 3½ hours. When the turkey is done, the joint between the leg and thigh bone will move easily when touched and a thermometer inserted in breast registers 170 degrees.

If desired, use the juices to make gravy, first skimming off the fat.

CRANBERRY RELISH:

With a vegetable peeler or a small, sharp knife, remove the zest but not the pith from a large orange and cut it into very thin julienne strips. Blanch the strips in boiling water for 1 minute, drain them in a sieve, and refresh them under running cold water.

In a saucepan, combine the sugar, water, and lemon juice. Bring the mixture to a boil over low heat, washing down any sugar crystals clinging to the sides of the pan with a brush dipped in cold water. Simmer the syrup for 5 minutes. Add cranberries and the orange strips and cook the mixture over moderately high heat for 4 to 5 minutes or until the berries have popped.

Let the mixture cool, then chill thoroughly. Makes about 3 cups.

Fran Stark was a beloved friend of many years. This is her recipe.

Fran's Yam Pudding

Boil and peel off the ends of the yams. Mash and add softened butter, brown sugar, cinnamon, cloves, nutmeg, and salt and pepper to taste. Then add the grated zest of the large orange, orange juice, brandy or bourbon, and the Cointreau.

Beat egg yolks in a bowl, then add the hot half-and-half and hot cream. Beat well and pour into yam mixture. Add melted butter.

Pour into greased baking dish. Cover the yams with marshmallows. Place in a bain-marie (a shallow pan of warm water) and cook at 350 degrees for about 1 hour. The marshmallows should be golden brown. Serves 6 to 8.

YAM PUDDING:

6 to 8 yams

10 tablespoons (1¼ sticks) butter, softened

½ cup brown sugar

1 teaspoon ground cinnamon

¼ teaspoon ground nutmeg

⅛ teaspoon ground cloves

salt and pepper

1 large orange

1 tablespoon orange juice

¼ cup brandy or bourbon

⅓ cup Cointreau

4 egg yolks

¼ cup hot half-and-half

¼ cup hot heavy cream

2 tablespoons melted butter

marshmallows

Bertie's Pecan Pie

FOR CRUST:

Pour flour into a bowl, add salt, then cut in shortening until the consistency is like corn meal. Sprinkle with water and mix with a fork by hand. Form into a round ball. May be refrigerated overnight if desired. Makes two 9-inch pie shells.

PECAN PIE:

Preheat oven to 350 degrees.

Beat eggs, sugar, salt, syrup, and butter with rotary beater. Stir in nuts. Roll out pie dough and press into 1 shell. Pour the mixture inside. Bake for 40 to 50 minutes.

CRUST:

2 cups sifted flour

1 teaspoon salt

¾ cup shortening

5 tablespoons ice water

PECAN PIE:

3 eggs

⅔ cup sugar

½ teaspoon salt

⅓ cup butter, melted

1 cup dark corn syrup

1 cup chopped pecan pieces

English Christmas Tea

JOAN RIVERS

Joan Rivers is best known as a popular television hostess, but when she has time, she loves to entertain. Her favorite occasion, and the one her friends look forward to every year, is the open house/English tea she hosts every Christmas for about 150 people. "I like to do this in the afternoon so people can just drop by and share best wishes," Joan said. "I fill the house with candles, holly, and other Christmas decor. It's very pretty and festive. Each guest receives a small gift, a token of my love and appreciation. I have much to be grateful for, and I am glad to have a chance to show this every year."

The menu for Joan's tea includes about eight different kinds of tea sandwiches, and wonderful cakes, including an incredible Yule Log, strawberry shortcake, and caramelized apple tart. She gave me the following recipes for the most popular sandwiches and for her cream scones. "All tea sandwiches should be thin and made as close to serving time as possible," Joan said. "If you make them ahead of time, wrap them in plastic wrap to keep the bread from drying out."

Cucumber Sandwiches

1 seedless cucumber, peeled and
    thinly sliced
white wine vinegar
white bread, thinly sliced
butter, softened
dill sprigs

Lay cucumber slices on a plate and sprinkle them lightly with vinegar. Cover for 30 minutes, then drain into a colander to remove excess liquid. Butter the bread slices, top with cucumber, then top with another bread slice. Trim off crust and cut each sandwich into triangles.

Smoked Salmon
and Chive Cream Cheese Sandwiches

smoked salmon, thinly sliced
black bread, thinly sliced
1/2 pound cream cheese,
    softened
2 tablespoons minced chives

Spread slices of bread with chive cream cheese, which is made by mixing cream cheese and chives. Top with smoked salmon and another piece of bread. Trim crust and cut into triangles.

Roast Beef and Horseradish Sandwiches

Spread slices of bread with horseradish mayonnaise, which is a mixture of mayonnaise and horseradish. Top with roast beef, red onion, and another slice of bread. Trim crust and cut into triangles.

rye bread, thinly sliced
$\frac{1}{2}$ cup lowfat mayonnaise
2 tablespoons prepared
  horseradish, drained
rare roast beef, thinly sliced
red onions, thinly sliced

Cream Scones

Preheat oven to 425 degrees.

In a large bowl, sift together the dry ingredients. Gradually add enough of the cream to form a soft dough. Knead lightly on a floured board, handling the dough gently to retain the air needed for the scones to rise.

Roll out to a $\frac{1}{2}$- to $\frac{3}{4}$-inch thickness. Cut into 2-inch rounds with a cookie cutter, and place on a cookie sheet, leaving a half-inch space around each one. Bake for 10 to 12 minutes or until golden brown.

Serve with strawberry jam and crème fraîche (see appendix, page 188). Yield: 12 to 16 scones.

SCONES:
2 cups flour
2 teaspoons sugar
1 teaspoon salt
1 teaspoon baking powder
1 cup heavy cream,
  approximately

Annual Christmas Party

BARBARA AND MARVIN DAVIS

Barbara and Marvin moved to Los Angeles from Denver when he owned the 20th Century Fox Film Studio. They have always entertained imaginatively. Their parties are the most original I've ever seen—and nothing compares with the annual Christmas party.

"We love to give a Christmas party," Barbara Davis told me, "because it's a time of good feelings of love and friendship, and a time when people share emotions and warm wishes. We decorate our house in Christmas themes, especially those related to children since Christmas is a holiday for children. We have plenty of Christmas songs with lots of children singing—children from all over the world, because that's the heart of the holiday spirit. It's fun to have teddy bears and toys and dolls and Christmas stockings as part of the decoration."

The Davis Christmas Party starts with a sumptuous hors d'oeuvres buffet and appetizers passed by waiters. It is followed by a formal dinner, and then as entertainment, a spectacular show.

The gathering begins around 8:00 P.M., with guests being seated for dinner at 9:00. The menu is varied, and the center-piece is Barbara's famous carrot soufflé, which has been shared and cooked by many of her friends.

M E N U

DINING ROOM TABLE BUFFET:
Cracked Crab, Shrimp, Oysters
Whole Scottish Smoked Salmon
Smoked Eastern Sturgeon
Country Pâté en Croute

PASSED BY WAITERS:
Petite Cheeseburgers
Chinese Dumplings
Shrimp Sauté Lemon Butter
Nachos with Chicken
Potato Pancakes with Apple Sauce & Sour Cream
Sweet & Sour Chicken Kabobs

DINNER:
Medallions of Fresh Lobster with Mustard/Mayonnaise Sauce
Cheese Toast

CHOICE OF:
Rack of Veal Chop Sauté
Roast Chicken

Fresh Asparagus with Leek
Pomme Soufflé in Potato Basket
* Carrot Soufflé

DESSERTS:
Florentine Shell Filled with Snowball
Hot Fudge Sauce
Christmas Cookies

Carrot Soufflé

Preheat oven to 350 degrees.

Purée carrots and eggs together, then add sugar, flour, vanilla, butter, and nutmeg. Pour into a buttered 1-quart soufflé dish and bake 40 minutes.

Mash together crushed corn flakes, brown sugar, and soft butter, then spread on top of soufflé. Bake for 5 to 10 minutes more. Serves 8 to 10.

1 pound fresh carrots, cooked (4 to 5 medium)
3 eggs
$1/3$ cup granulated sugar
3 tablespoons flour
1 teaspoon vanilla
$1/4$ pound (1 stick) butter, melted
dash nutmeg
$1/4$ to $1/2$ cup crushed cornflakes
3 tablespoons brown sugar
2 tablespoons soft butter

New Year's Eve in Palm Beach

JUDITH AND ALFRED TAUBMAN

*E*very New Year's Eve, the Taubmans host a party at their Palm Beach house and invite family and friends. A buffet dinner is served prior to the "Coconuts" (a local bachelor's dance).

Alfred, a great entrepreneur, owns the famous international auction house, Sotheby's, and he is always on the run. Judy reminds me of the saying that the busiest people always have the most time to give. They have hosted some of the loveliest dinners I've ever been to.

Judy says the secret to her success is very simple: "Good food, good wine, and a good mixture of guests. This ensures that everyone is happy and high spirited. I believe that the atmosphere is created by careful planning and attention to every detail—from the flowers to the soft lighting to the delectable chocolates and nuts dotted everywhere on every table throughout the house.

"When serving a buffet, I always make sure that the table is constantly replenished with fresh platters. Even after one hour, the buffet table looks as beautiful and inviting as when it is first presented.

"The key element to any party's success is, of course, the people. We invite our friends and I ask my daughter Tiffany to invite hers, too. The blend is very pleasing to both generations and it makes for a more lively party."

M E N U

* Pesto Cheese Straws
* Tiropitas
Borekas
Homemade Brioche
Assorted Breads
Twice-Baked Potato Halves with Caviar
* Moussaka
Honey-Glazed Ham with Mustard and Cloves
Beef Croquettes
Smoked Norwegian Salmon
Pâté de Foie Gras
Wild Duck Pâté
Salad Haricots Verts
Assorted Mustards

Pesto Cheese Straws

CHEESE STRAWS:

1 package (17 ¼ ounces) frozen puff pastry sheets; thaw ahead

1 cup grated Parmesan cheese

2 cups pesto sauce (prepared or homemade)

Lay out puff pastry sheet. Sprinkle Parmesan cheese over pastry and roll cheese into the pastry sheet with a rolling pin. Spread pesto sauce on one-half of the pastry sheet. Fold pastry edge-to-edge lengthwise and cut into strips ½ x 4-inches long. Twist strips at the ends to form a spiral. Place on a cookie sheet and freeze prior to baking.

Preheat oven to 375 degrees.

Bake for approximately 7 minutes until brown. Makes about 24 straws.

Tiropitas

TIROPITAS:

1 package (16 ounces) frozen phyllo dough; thaw ahead

½ pound (2 sticks) butter

1 cup extra virgin olive oil

FILLING:

12 ounces feta cheese

4 ounces Kasseri cheese

1 egg

1 teaspoon fresh, crushed garlic

Mix filling ingredients together in a food processor until smooth. Let set in refrigerator for 24 hours.

Preheat oven to 325 degrees.

Melt butter and mix with olive oil. Lay out 1 sheet of phyllo dough and brush with butter and olive oil mixture. Put a second layer of phyllo dough on top and brush with butter and olive oil. Place third sheet of dough on top and brush again with butter and olive oil mixture. Cut dough into 6 equal long strips.

Place filling on upper left corner of each strip and fold down to create a triangle. Cut. Continue folding back and forth (like folding an American flag) to the end of the strip. Repeat until all ingredients are used.

Bake for 10 minutes until lightly brown. Yield: About 48 triangular pieces.

Moussaka

Slice eggplant lengthwise into $\frac{1}{4}$-inch-thick slices and soak in milk for 1 hour to remove bitterness. Finely chop onions, shallots, and garlic in food processor. Sauté this mixture in $\frac{1}{4}$ cup of olive oil until the onions are translucent. Season with pepper, oregano, and cinnamon. Add ground lamb and sauté until brown. Drain off the excess fat, add tomatoes, and simmer uncovered for 20 minutes. Remove from heat and add Parmesan cheese and bread crumbs. Set aside for later.

Drain eggplant and discard milk. In a separate skillet, sauté eggplant slices in olive oil until lightly brown. Remove and drain.

In a casserole dish, assemble in layers. Place 1 layer of eggplant on the bottom, then add one layer of meat mixture on top. Repeat layering 3 times, ending with a layer of meat on top.

Pour Sauce Béchamel on top and poke holes with a fork, allowing sauce to seep through. Bake for 1 hour at 350 degrees until eggplant is tender. Test with a fork.

Ingredients:

- 4 large eggplants
- 1 quart milk
- 3 small onions
- 6 bunches shallots
- 2 large cloves garlic
- $\frac{1}{4}$ cup olive oil, plus more for frying eggplant
- 1 tablespoon ground black pepper
- 2 tablespoons ground oregano
- 1 tablespoon ground cinnamon
- 4 pounds ground lamb
- 1 quart diced, skinless tomatoes
- $\frac{1}{2}$ cup Parmesan cheese
- $\frac{1}{4}$ cup bread crumbs
- 1 quart Sauce Béchamel

SAUCE BECHAMEL:

Melt butter in saucepan and stir in flour to paste-like consistency. Slowly whisk in milk and stir until thick. Add bay leaf, cayenne pepper, and nutmeg. Simmer uncovered for 5 minutes. Remove bay leaf.

SAUCE:

- 4 tablespoons ($\frac{1}{2}$ stick) butter
- $\frac{1}{2}$ cup all-purpose flour
- 4 cups milk
- 1 bay leaf
- 1 teaspoon cayenne pepper
- 1 teaspoon freshly ground nutmeg

CHAPTER SIX

Favorite Recipes From Friends

AN ECLECTIC SELECTION FROM AROUND THE WORLD

I am truly lucky to know so many wonderful and interesting people. Their input has enriched my life, and I'm delighted to pass on their thoughts and recipes to you.

I believe there is no such thing as a completely "original" recipe—and that's part of what makes this process so fascinating. Recipes are passed on from mother to daughter and from friend to friend. As they gather history, they often change form, with individuals adding their own special touches.

There is nothing quite so generous as sharing a treasured recipe—of whispering that long-held secret ingredient. It's quite a gift. I know of people who have jealously guarded recipes all the way to the grave! A friend told me the story of two women she knew who were close in every way but one—sharing recipes. There was a dish in particular that one woman had been trying to coax out of her friend for forty years, to no avail. She tried to prepare it on her own, but it never quite worked and she couldn't figure out the missing ingredient.

It so happens that her friend became ill and she knew she was dying. As she lay in bed, almost too weak to speak, she motioned for the woman to lean close, and whispered with what was practically her dying breath, "Cinnamon."

In this chapter, many of my friends from all over have given me their prized recipes. They represent a variety of cultures, regions, lifestyles, and tastes, and in themselves comprise one of the best cookbooks one can imagine. Since the men and women who have supplied recipes are themselves so interesting, I'll tell you a little bit about them as well.

SOUPS & STEWS

Texas Chili
Walnut Soup

🐌

NANCY HAMON

Someone once said of Nancy Hamon that if you know anyone from Texas, it's likely to be Nancy. When her husband Jake was alive, their Dallas home was open to a constant variety of guests. Even now, Nancy entertains frequently. To me, she represents what Texas is all about—its warm, friendly, embracing style. These days, at casual dinners, Nancy often serves her Texas Chili.

Texas Chili

CHILI:

5 or 6 cloves garlic

1 large yellow onion

2 cups water, divided

2 pounds lean ground chuck or venison

1 can (6 ounces) tomato paste

2 teaspoons cilantro leaves or coriander

1 tablespoon dried marjoram

1 tablespoon dried oregano

1 heaping tablespoon ground cumin

2 ounces chili powder (6 tablespoons plus 2 teaspoons)

salt

Pour boiling water over the garlic cloves and peel them. Slice onion. Place garlic and onion in a blender with a cup of water. Chop coarsely.

In a heavy pot, brown meat well, then add the onion/garlic mixture and the rest of the ingredients. Simmer covered for at least 1¹/₂ hours; add salt to taste. Serves 6 to 8.

🐌

MARION (MRS. EARLE) JORGENSEN

When you meet Marion Jorgensen and her husband Earle, you know what it means to grow older but get younger every day. Marion is a role model for every woman—energetic, curious, and always challenged by life. I think she's found the Fountain of Youth. Marion and Earle entertain frequently in their house in Los Angeles. Marion has served her Walnut Soup to rave reviews for many years.

Walnut Soup

Put the walnuts between two sheets of waxed paper and crush them with a rolling pin.

Place the stock in a saucepan and bring to a boil.

Place the butter and flour in a small bowl and mix well. Add a little of the boiling stock and mix well. Pour this into the stock and bring to a boil, stirring constantly.

Place the egg yolks and seasonings in a small bowl and beat with a fork.

Pour a little of the stock over this and mix well, then add to the hot soup and stir well.

Do not allow to boil after adding the egg yolks.

Just before serving, mix together the nuts, sour cream, and chives, and add to the soup. Serves 6.

1 cup fresh shelled walnuts
3 cups homemade chicken stock
2 tablespoons butter
2 tablespoons flour
2 egg yolks
¼ teaspoon salt
⅛ teaspoon pepper
6 tablespoons sour cream (at room temperature)
1 tablespoon chopped fresh chives

FIRST AND MAIN COURSES

Lebanese Mouloukish
Sour Cream Soufflé
Salmon Duke of Bedford
Blanquette de Veau Nicole
Eggs Surprise
Chicken Cynthia
Zucchini Casserole
Aunt Jo's Tacos
Lobster in Coconut
Steak and Kidney Pie
Chicken Paprika
Rehrucken Andreas
Leg of Lamb
Penne à la Vodka
Texan Tamale Pie
Lamb Chops á Ma Facon
Filet of Sole Grimaldi
Caviar Tart
Crab Isabelle

MOUNA (MRS. NASSER) AL-RASHID

*W*hen Mouna visits Los Angeles, I feel as though I've been swept into a whirlwind of activity. My beautiful young Lebanese friend never stops urging me to try new adventures—even disco dancing until two in the morning! You'd never suspect that she is the mother of five children, or that she lives in Riyadh, Saudi Arabia, where women are seen and not heard. Mouna has managed to avoid being defined by either her great wealth or the stringencies of her culture. She's just herself—and I am delighted that she has made me her friend. She prepared this recipe for me recently when I visited her and her children in Greece. It is absolutely delicious.

"This is a complicated dish," she warned, "but worth the effort. I inherited it from my mother who inherited it from hers. My grandmother was famous for it, then my mother, now me. It came to be our Sunday family lunch.

"My grandmother was so proud of this recipe that if anyone happened to be at her table on Sunday and didn't eat, she would literally throw him out. Believe me, it's true. Those unfortunates who didn't like it were forced to wait in her olive garden during the meal.

"Mouloukish is a green plant that looks like spinach but has a distinct flavor."

Lebanese Mouloukish

MOULOUKISH:

2 pounds mouloukish (saloyot, a Philippine version, can be found in Oriental markets)

¾ pound fresh coriander leaves (cilantro)

½ pound garlic (5 to 6 heads)

3 tablespoons salt, divided

½ pound (2 sticks) butter

2 pounds onions

1 cup corn oil

2 pounds chicken or rabbit meat
water to cook meat

¼ pound cinnamon sticks, divided (20 to 24 sticks)

4 slices lemon, divided

2 pounds lamb meat with bones

1 teaspoon pepper

4 cups white rice, uncooked

¼ pound roasted pita bread, cut into small pieces

Separate mouloukish leaves from the stems and wash thoroughly in cold water. Lay overnight on a white linen cloth to dry. In the morning, cut the leaves very small and set aside.

Separate cilantro leaves from stems one by one and wash thoroughly.

Prepare garlic by peeling it. Mix garlic and coriander leaves and mash with 1 tablespoon of salt until it forms a paste. Fry the mixture in butter.

Cut the onions into very small pieces and fry in corn oil.

Boil the chicken or rabbit in water with half the cinnamon sticks, 2 slices of lemon, and 1 tablespoon of salt, until it is cooked. Reserve the broth.

Boil lamb in water with the remaining cinnamon sticks, 2 slices of lemon, and 1 tablespoon of salt until it is cooked. Reserve the broth. Put chicken and lamb, after separating from the bone, in a pan in the oven for roasting and browning on top.

Take the lamb broth and pour it over the fried onions. Boil for 5 minutes.

Add the garlic/coriander mixture. Boil for 5 more minutes. Add salt and pepper to taste.

Add the mouloukish leaves. Boil for 10 more minutes.

Cook the rice in the broth the chicken was cooked in; salt if needed.

SAUCE:

Cut the onions into very small pieces. Mix one half with the lemon juice and one half with the vinegar.

Place in a deep dish in this order: first the rice, then the meat, then the mouloukish. Serve the sauce separately, and eat with small pieces of toasted pita bread. Serves 20.

SAUCE:
1 pound onions
2 cups lemon juice
2 cups vinegar

28.

BILL BLASS

Bill Blass has many friends and he's a very warm and jovial host. He once told me that with his frantic lifestyle, he considers cooking to be therapeutic. His philosophy of entertaining is simple: "The secret of entertaining is the desire to do so," he told me. "Never entertain if you are not in the mood for it."

Bill's favorite event is Christmas Eve. "I always spend it in the country," he says, "and the house looks polished without being consumed by Christmas decorations. I put the tree in one room, and the rest of the house may be full of spring flowers. I like people to bring their children so there is a variety of ages as well.

"This Christmas Eve, the wonderful singer Jessye Norman led us in Christmas carols after dinner, although no one wanted to sing, preferring just to listen to her sing the familiar carols in German, Italian, French, and English.

"The sour cream soufflé is always a favorite dish of mine. I serve it as a main course for lunch with smoked trout or smoked salmon, thin slices of brown bread, and a salad."

Sour Cream Soufflé

½ cup freshly grated Parmesan
    cheese
1½ cups sour cream
½ cup sifted flour
5 eggs, separated, plus 2 extra
    egg whites
1 generous teaspoon salt
¼ teaspoon cayenne pepper
2 tablespoons chopped fresh
    chives

Preheat oven to 350 degrees.

Butter a 2-quart souffle dish, coat with Parmesan cheese, and refrigerate. Pour the sour cream into a bowl and sift flour into sour cream. Thoroughly whip together with a wire whisk. Add yolks one at a time, whipping briskly after each addition. Then stir in the salt, pepper, chives, and remaining cheese. Beat egg whites until they hold firm, shiny peaks when the beater is held up straight. Gently fold into egg mixture with a rubber spatula. Place in oven and bake for 30 to 35 minutes. Serves 6 to 8.

❧

NICOLE, DUCHESS OF BEDFORD

The Duke and Duchess of Bedford, Ian and Nicole, are delightful people who entertain beautifully. The key, says Nicole, is for everyone to have a wonderful time. As she told me bluntly, "One should invite the most interesting and intelligent guests. Never invite bores or fools out of pity or kindness. If you must, invite them alone or with trusted friends, but never to a party, as they make no effort and drag the others down. I personally only invite friends I love or like very much or who make me laugh or have a sharp wit. I have been known to say, 'Come, but don't bring your wife/husband' if I know the person has a chip on his shoulder. Ian says I'm rude, but I simply feel life is too short to waste it with people who bring you down."

Ian and Nicole gave me the following recipes for their favorite fish and meat courses.

Salmon Duke of Bedford

SALMON:
½ cup wine or malt vinegar
2 cups white wine
6 peppercorns
1 teaspoon dried fennel seeds
about 20 coriander seeds
2 bay leaves
small sprig of fresh thyme
3 large carrots, sliced
2 onions, sliced
1 fresh Scottish salmon, about 6
    pounds, cleaned
1 potato
2 lemons
tomato, cucumber, and lettuce
    for garnish
¼ pound (1 stick) butter, chilled
finely chopped onion
chopped fresh parsley
tarragon
mayonnaise

In a salmon kettle or large saucepan, pour the vinegar and white wine. Add the peppercorns, fennel seeds, a few coriander seeds, the bay leaves, thyme, sliced carrots, and onion. Fill with water and boil the mixture.

Scale the salmon and place it on a clean white cloth. Place a potato between its teeth and wrap the cloth around it, tying it at both ends.

When the liquid is boiling, place the salmon (wrapped) in the water and simmer for approximately 1 hour, depending on the size of the salmon.

Remove salmon from the water and open the cloth. Test by touching the flesh with your fingers. If cooked, the flesh will feel soft to the touch.

Remove skin, leaving the head intact. Decorate with lemon, tomato, and cucumber on a bed of lettuce. Use piped butter to bring out the features of the head.

Remove potato from the teeth and replace with lemon.

Serve with green mayonnaise, which can be made by adding finely chopped onion, chopped parsley and tarragon to ordinary mayonnaise. Serves 10.

Blanquette de Veau Nicole

Squeeze lemon over veal and place in a pot. Fill the pot with cold water, covering the meat. Add carrots, onions, garlic, laurel leaf, thyme, salt and pepper. Bring to a boil, cover and simmer on low heat for 1½ hours. Skim from time to time.

SAUCE:

Place butter in saucepan, add flour, and mix rapidly with a wooden spoon. Remove saucepan from the burner, and add a ladleful of stock.

Return saucepan to the burner and cook rapidly on medium heat, adding stock (4 to 5 ladles) to make the sauce the consistency of custard.

Break the egg yolk into the cream. Add this mixture to the sauce gently, on low heat.

Drain excess stock from the veal and add sauce. Simmer very slowly until serving. Serves 6 to 8.

1 lemon, juice only
2½ pounds veal
6 medium carrots
6 medium onions
2 cloves garlic
1 laurel (bay) leaf
1 small bunch thyme
salt and pepper

SAUCE:
1 tablespoon butter
1 tablespoon flour
1 egg yolk
3 tablespoons cream

ès

MARCELA (MRS. JAVIER) PEREZ DE CUELLAR

Marcela is the Peruvian wife of the former Secretary General of the United Nations. As such, she has entertained leaders from all over the world.

Marcela told me, "I prefer to give luncheons. People are more relaxed and it seems to me that they enjoy it much more that time of day. Once we even had music, we ended up dancing, and let me tell you, my guests were very busy people. They left the house like they had had an unexpected holiday.

"I love to make this recipe for lunch. Everyone enjoys it. "

Eggs Surprise

Make crepes with your favorite recipe, but don't cook them too much. The quantity depends on the number of guests.

Cut mushrooms into small pieces and fry them in butter, adding a pinch of salt and pepper. Fry some bacon and cut it into very small pieces.

Arrange each crepe in a cup and fill it with an egg, mushroom pieces, and bacon. Take the borders of the crepe and fold them into a package, tying with a piece of string. Remove the crepe from the cup very carefully.

When you have the amount you want, fry them in a pot of very hot oil until they are crispy on the outside. Remove from the oil and dry on paper towels.

Pass the green part of scallions through boiling water, then cool. Replace the strings with the scallion and tie them like a bow.

Serve with hollandaise sauce.

ès

MARION (MRS. EARLE) JORGENSEN

This dish is another favorite of Marion's:

Chicken Cynthia

Combine 6 tablespoons of the flour and the seasonings and roll the breasts in the mixture.

Heat 6 tablespoons of the butter or margarine in a large skillet, and brown the breasts very lightly on both sides. Lower the heat and cook gently for 10 minutes.

Sprinkle with the onion, add the white wine, and bring to a boil. Cover the pan tightly. Simmer over very low heat or bake at 350 degrees for 20 minutes.

Work the remaining 2 tablespoons flour and 4 tablespoons butter together in a bowl with a fork. Add the hot chicken stock and mix well.

Add mixture to the chicken, then add the lemon juice, curaçao, and sherry. Cover and cook 15 to 20 minutes longer.

While the chicken is cooking, peel and section the oranges and place them in a warm place so they won't be cold when put on the platter.

To serve, place the chicken on a heated platter and surround it with the washed and drained grapes and the orange sections. Place one cluster of grapes in the center of the chicken. Serves 8.

CHICKEN CYNTHIA:

8 tablespoons flour, divided

2 teaspoons salt

$\frac{1}{2}$ teaspoon pepper

$\frac{1}{4}$ teaspoon paprika

4 large chicken breasts—skinless, boneless, cut in half

10 tablespoons butter or margarine, divided

2 tablespoons peeled, chopped onion

1 cup dry white wine

1$\frac{1}{2}$ cups hot chicken stock

1 tablespoon lemon juice

2 tablespoons curaçao

2 tablespoons sherry

2 oranges, peeled and sectioned

$\frac{1}{4}$ pound seedless grapes

❧

CATIE (MRS. DONALD) MARRON

Catie is a talented senior editor of *Vogue* magazine, and is married to Donald, the tall, handsome head of Paine Webber Inc., the stock brokerage firm.

Catie said, "To me, the best dinner party is when the guests call up the next day to say what a great time they had, how much they loved their dinner partners, and how casual and relaxed the evening was (hopefully not seeing all the hidden effort that goes into a successful and relaxed party).

"I try to make the rooms and table settings as beautiful as possible, without looking overly formal or stiff. I spend a lot of time thinking about all the elements—the guest list, the menu, the table settings, the seating plan, the flowers. I always vary the flowers and have certain favorites for each season. I especially love to use viburnum with peonies or roses in spring, dahlias in late summer, and ranunculus in fall.

"I always try to serve something a bit unexpected or different at every meal. One of my favorites is this Zucchini Casserole. It was always a secret recipe—until now!"

Zucchini Casserole

8 medium zucchini

unsalted butter to sauté

2 large onions, finely sliced

flour

$^1\!/_2$ cup heavy cream

6 to 8 ounces grated Swiss cheese
    (1$^1\!/_2$ to 2 cups)

$^1\!/_2$ cup Parmesan cheese

flavored bread crumbs

salt and pepper

Scrub and medium-grate the zucchini. Place in a colander, salt, and squeeze out the excess water by hand.

Melt butter in a sauté pan and sauté the onions.

Remove and put in a bowl. With additional butter, sauté the zucchini a handful at a time. While sautéing, sprinkle with flour and add enough of the cream to bind. Zucchini sticks easily so take care.

Place zucchini in a bowl with the onions and mix them together. Add the grated Swiss cheese and mix. Add the Parmesan cheese and mix. Add enough heavy cream to moisten, salt lightly, and liberally add finely grated or powdered pepper.

Pour the mixture into a buttered soufflé dish and sprinkle the top with flavored bread crumbs.

Bake at 350 degrees until firm, bubbling and golden brown—about 45 minutes. Serves 8 to 10.

&

AILEEN MEHLE

Aileen is best known to millions of readers as "Suzy," the great society columnist. Although she spends most of her life attending formal dinners, charity events, and other social doings, at home Aileen welcomes an opportunity to be casual.

"This is a recipe for my Aunt Jo's sloppy, messy, get-out-the-paper-towels tacos," she explained. "I remember loving them from my childhood, and still do. Aunt Jo, who is unfortunately no longer with us, was born in Minneapolis, which isn't exactly taco country. But when she moved to California as a young girl, she was fascinated by Tex-Mex, Cal-Mex food. She put her own special spin on these tacos, the main difference being that she fried them after they were stuffed.

"This recipe serves eight, allowing three tacos per person. If there are any left over, which there rarely are, they are even better warmed up the next day. You can forget about the cholesterol level, but if you're a taco addict like me, it's worth it!"

Aunt Jo's Tacos

Two large skillets are needed—one to cook the meat, the other to fry the tacos.

In one skillet, crumble and brown the meat. Add the red chili sauce and green chilies. Simmer until moisture soaks into the meat and liquid reduces to almost dry. Using a slotted spoon, fill each taco with 2 tablespoons of meat mixture, grated cheese, and lettuce. Fold tortilla over and fry in ½ inch of oil for 2 or 3 minutes on each side until well-browned. Use a spatula to turn the tortillas, and a large, long-handled spoon to hold them together while they're frying. Remove and drain on paper towels.

2 pounds lean ground beef
2 cans (10 ounces each) Las Palmas red chili or enchilada sauce
1 can (4 ounces) chopped green chilies
salt and garlic salt (optional)
1½ cups sharp cheddar cheese, grated
2 cups shredded iceberg lettuce
24 corn tortillas
vegetable oil

ETTI PLESCH

Since her husband Arpad died, Etti has made her place in the great international cities—Paris, New York, London, and Monte Carlo. This lovely Austrian woman is a "femme fatale" who can charm birds off the trees—as I'm sure her seven husbands would agree. When she was younger, Etti would run enormous houses, but now she maintains a simpler life and, like so many of us, does much of her entertaining in restaurants. This is a recipe she serves at home in Monte Carlo. It is a simple dish which utilizes a coconut as a pressure cooker.

Lobster in Coconut

Remove the top of the coconut and scrape out some of the nut. Remove the juice. Mince the nut.

Fill coconut shell with lobster (or, if you prefer, chicken) and add the minced nut and juice.

Seal the top of the coconut with pastry around it and bake in the oven for 20 minutes. Remove the top and serve the mixture in the coconut.

COUNTESS OF CHAMBRUN

Raine is the daughter of Barbara Cartland, the widow of Earl Spencer, former stepmother of Princess Diana of Wales, and now the Countess of Chambrun. We met many years ago at the American Embassy in London when Walter Annenberg was ambassador. I remember so well the first time I saw her. This marvelous apparition swept into the room with glorious red hair and a gown of black velvet. She came straight over to me and said, "Oh, Betsy, I feel that I know you." Then she said they were visiting Los Angeles soon and before I knew it, I had arranged for them to stay in my house. Today, we visit whenever either of us is in the other's country. She was kind enough to give me her family recipe for traditional Steak and Kidney Pie.

Steak and Kidney Pie

1 pound stewing beef

5 ounces beef or lamb kidneys

1½ tablespoons fat

2 tablespoons flour, seasoned with salt and pepper

2 ounces (⅓ cup) chopped onions, optional

Worcestershire sauce

1 bay leaf

1 tablespoon chopped fresh parsley

2 tablespoons herbes de provence

1 cup beef stock

6 ounces puff pastry

1 egg for glaze

Cut beef into 2 ¾-inch pieces, discarding any fat or gristle. Skin and decore the kidneys and cut in half. Refrigerate kidneys.

Heat the fat in a heavy-based pan until hot, and brown beef, stirring in the flour and onions and cooking to a light brown color. Add a few sprinkles of Worcestershire sauce, the bay leaf, parsley, mixed herbs, and beef stock.

Bring to a boil and then simmer for 1½ to 2 hours or until meat is tender. Forty minutes before cooking is completed, add the kidneys.

When cooked, remove the bay leaf, taste for seasonings, and correct. Place in a 3-quart pie dish. Cover carefully with a puff pastry top, pressing it down tightly. Beat egg lightly with fork. Brush over top of pastry.

Bake 20 to 25 minutes at 400 degrees. Serves 4 to 6.

IVANA TRUMP

*I*vana, the glamorous former wife of Donald Trump, now a published author and businesswoman, told me, "One of my favorite occasions is my Girlfriends Spa Weekend at Mar-A-Lago, in Palm Beach, Florida, where we combine exercise, great food, and relaxation—for the tune-up of mind and body." During the weekend, Ivana serves her Chicken Paprika, a recipe she brought from her childhood in Czechoslovakia.

Chicken Paprika

Disjoint chicken and dust with ¹/₂ cup flour seasoned with salt, white pepper, and 1¹/₂ teaspoons Hungarian paprika.

Melt the butter and vegetable oil in a heavy saucepan, then sauté chicken until brown. Remove.

Add onion and the remaining 2 tablespoons of Hungarian paprika to the pan. When onions are translucent, return chicken to the pan and add chicken stock. Simmer covered until tender—about 1 hour.

Stir together remaining 2 tablespoons flour and sour cream and add slowly to the pot. Simmer until thickened and smooth. Do not boil or sour cream might separate.

Serve with noodles or rice. Serves 4.

1 frying chicken (about 2¹/₂ pounds)
¹/₂ cup plus 2 tablespoons flour, divided
¹/₂ teaspoon salt
¹/₂ teaspoon white pepper
2¹/₂ tablespoons sweet Hungarian paprika, divided
1¹/₂ tablespoons butter
1¹/₂ tablespoons vegetable oil
1 cup finely chopped yellow onion
2 cups seasoned chicken stock
1 cup cultured sour cream
rice or noodles

H.S.H. PRINCESS GLORIA VON THURN UND TAXIS

*A*s I described earlier, I was fortunate to spend one Easter in Regensburg, Germany with the Thurn und Taxis. It was quite wonderful. Now that Johannes has died, Gloria entertains less spectacularly, but there are certain dishes, like this saddle of venison, that often appear on her table.

Rehrucken Andreas
(Saddle of Venison Andreas)

saddle of venison
bottle of red wine, divided
1 cup Calvados (apple brandy)
2 ounces ($\frac{1}{4}$ cup) brandy
3 bay leaves
6 juniper berries
4 peppercorns
3 sprigs fresh tarragon
3 sprigs fresh dill
larding pork
$\frac{1}{4}$ pound (1 stick) melted butter
2 cups sour cream, warmed
1 tablespoon flour
salt

MUSHROOM CAPS:
24 mushroom caps
2 tablespoons butter, plus more
   to sauté
$\frac{1}{2}$ lemon, juice only
$\frac{1}{2}$ cup goose liver pâté
24 walnut halves
meat glaze

Marinate a well-aged, full-length saddle of venison for 24 hours in a mixture of red wine (reserve $\frac{1}{2}$ cup), Calvados, brandy, bay leaves, juniper berries, peppercorns, tarragon, and dill. Drain and reserve marinade.

Lard venison in 2 double rows with strips of larding pork, and lay a braid of larding pork strips along the spine.

Strain the reserved marinade. Roast the saddle in a 500-degree oven for 5 minutes. Reduce the heat to 450 degrees and roast for 1 hour, basting every 5 minutes with melted butter and pan juices. Reduce the heat to 400 degrees and continue roasting until it is done to taste, about 30 minutes, basting every 10 minutes.

Place the saddle on a hot platter and keep it hot. Pour off all but $\frac{1}{2}$ cup of the pan juices. Place the pan over low heat and add 1 cup of the strained marinade, $\frac{1}{2}$ cup of red wine, and 2 cups of warm sour cream into which 1 tablespoon of flour has been stirred. Cook, stirring constantly, until the sauce is smooth. Add salt to taste. Serve sauce separately.

Serve mushroom caps on the side: Simmer mushroom caps in salted water to cover, with butter and the lemon juice, until they are tender—about 10 minutes. Drain and fill each cap with 1 teaspoon goose liver pâté. Lay on top of each a walnut half that has been sautéed in butter and brushed with meat glaze.

Accompany with potato dumplings, red cabbage with apples, and stewed lingonberries sprinkled with slivered orange rind.

&

CONNIE WALD

*C*onnie is the widow of Jerry Wald, the famous Warner Brothers producer who did such memorable films as *Mildred Pierce*, *Peyton Place*, and *Key Largo*. Connie is famous in her own right for being a great Hollywood hostess.

Anyone who has come in contact with Connie over the years has loved her. She's one of those women who always has a happy word for everyone. She's especially known for her "fall down dinners," which means casual and relaxed. Even her Leg of Lamb is easy to make, and it's the best.

Leg of Lamb

Cover lamb with butter and rosemary and pat on solidly. Insert slices of garlic and cook at 450 degrees for 15 minutes. Reduce heat to 350 degrees and cook for 1 hour. Slice parallel to the bone.

leg of lamb, most of skin
    removed
butter
fresh rosemary
sliced garlic

Penne à la Vodka

Melt butter, add pepper flakes, and heat thoroughly. Add vodka and heat thoroughly. Add tomato sauce and heat thoroughly. Add cream and heat thoroughly.

Meanwhile, cook pasta. When ready, combine pasta with sauce and mix in Parmesan cheese. Serve immediately with extra cheese on the side. Serves 6 to 8.

$1/4$ pound (1 stick) unsalted butter
1 teaspoon red pepper flakes
1 cup vodka
1 cup tomato sauce
1 cup heavy cream
1 cup Parmesan cheese
1 box (16 ounces) de Cecco or
    other penne pasta

ﺰ

LYNN (MRS. OSCAR) WYATT

Lynn is a classic and glamourous Texas belle from Houston who is well known, among her other accomplishments, for the birthday party she gives every July at her home in the South of France. Each year, the party has a different theme. The dinner is always seated, with tables set up in the garden or around the pool. There is live music and a lively guest list composed of people from all over the world. The tables, flowers, and decorations reflect the theme, but the menu remains the same, and there's one dish in particular that is served to great praise every year: Lynn's Texan Tamale Pie, a recipe that has been in her family for many years.

Texan Tamale Pie

18 corn tortillas, divided

1½ pounds ground beef

¾ cup chopped onions

1 teaspoon salt

2 tablespoons corn flour (masa)

1½ teaspoons chili powder

1 can (16 ounces) tomatoes, broken up

1 can (8 ounces) tomato sauce

1 cup whole kernel corn

1 tablespoon fresh chopped cilantro

2 cups shredded cheddar cheese, divided

Line a 3-quart casserole (bottom and sides) with corn tortillas (approximately 6). Sauté beef and onions until the beef is brown and crumbly. Pour off excess grease. Stir in salt, flour, and chili powder. Add the broken tomatoes, tomato sauce, and corn. Cook slowly for 15 minutes. Add the fresh chopped cilantro and continue cooking for 15 minutes more.

Preheat oven to 350 degrees.

Add one half of the beef mixture to the casserole, and layer ½ cup of cheese and a layer of tortillas. Repeat for a second layer. Spread the remaining cup of cheese on top and cover with foil.

Bake for 30 minutes. Remove the foil and cook for 15 minutes more, until cheese is melted and slightly brown. Serves 6 to 8.

CECILE (MRS. EZRA) ZILKHA

*C*ecile Zilkha is the lovely Iranian wife of a prominent New York banker. She and Ezra make their home in Paris, Southampton, Long Island, and New York City, where Cecile organizes spectacular fund-raising events for the Metropolitan Opera.

Cecile is a delightful hostess—charming, petite, and gracious. She always serves wonderfully different food with a Middle Eastern touch. When she entertains, she pays special attention to the mix and the seating arrangement of her guests. She told me, "I have found that when I do my seating plan, if I seat a guest between someone whom they do not know well and someone whom they know, they have a much better time. It's always fun to meet new people." These lamb chops are a specialty of hers.

Lamb Chops à Ma Façon

LAMB CHOPS:

½ pound pâté de foie gras, divided

6 double lamb chops with 1 bone per chop, trimmed of all fat

1 pound phyllo pastry dough

½ pound (2 sticks) melted butter or substitute, divided

¼ pound morel mushrooms, or any kind preferred

½ cup port wine

Preheat oven to 375 degrees.

Spread a slice of foie gras on each lamb chop.

Wrap each chop separately in phyllo dough that has been cut into large squares and brushed lightly with melted butter. Leave the bone unwrapped.

Place chops in a buttered ovenware dish and bake until the dough is golden brown—approximately 30 to 40 minutes.

Accompany the chops with this sauce: Sauté mushrooms in remaining butter, add remaining foie gras, and stir until smooth. Add port wine and bring to a boil, stirring constantly. Serve in a sauce boat. Serves 6.

෬

BARON ALEXIS DE REDE

*B*aron de Rede is a charming Frenchman of great taste who lives in the Hotel Lambert in Paris. It was there that he gave his fabulous Oriental Ball, of which I spoke earlier, and served this wonderful dish.

Fillet of Sole Grimaldi

In salted boiling water, cook the macaroni al dente. When cooked, place it on a heatproof plate and add heavy cream and sliced truffle. Set aside.

In the same pot, reduce the truffle juice and fish stock by half. Then add 2 tablespoons butter and stir until it is well mixed. Add salt and pepper and set aside.

Place the macaroni mixture in a 300-degree oven and cook it for 15 minutes.

In a sauté pan, cook the sole with butter and oil—2 minutes for each side or until it flakes. Place the sole on top of the macaroni mixture and add the sauce. Garnish with tips of chervil and serve immediately. Serves 4.

8 ounces (scant 2 cups) macaroni
3 tablespoons heavy cream
1 truffle, sliced
6 ounces ($^3/_4$ cup) truffle juice
2 ounces ($^1/_4$ cup) fish stock
2 tablespoons butter, plus more for sautéing
salt and pepper
2 fillet of sole, cleaned and deboned, cut in half
vegetable oil
1 bunch chervil

෬

JEROME ZIPKIN

*J*erome, known to his friends as Jerry, has been a family friend for years. Although he's known for his acid tongue, Jerry is very charming, and he's an impeccable host.

He sometimes serves this Caviar Tart instead of a variety of canapés. Once he served it at a birthday party with a lighted candle in the center. It's not only delicious, but with the three colors of caviar, it makes a striking presentation.

Caviar Tart

Line a puff pastry shell with crème fraîche (see appendix, page 188). Pre-cut tart into pie-shaped wedges and sprinkle with chopped chives.

Fill three pastry bags with black, golden, and red caviar. Pipe the caviars onto the crème fraîche in concentric circles, beginning with a solid circle of black in the center of the tart.

Decorate the edges of the tart with thinly sliced lemon half-moons and finely chopped parsley.

🐌

KENNETH JAY LANE

Kenny Lane is famous the world over for his fabulous costume jewelry. His cozy lunches at home are almost as famous and an eagerly sought-after invitation. He served this crab dish one day when I was there and I begged for the recipe.

Crab Isabelle

CRAB ISABELLE:

1 red bell pepper, chopped

1/2 cup chopped white onion

1 tablespoon butter

2 pounds fresh lump Maryland crabmeat (at room temperature)

1/4 cup chopped Italian parsley

2 eggs, lightly beaten

2 tablespoons Dijon mustard

1 tablespoon lemon juice

1/2 teaspoon Worcestershire sauce

1/4 teaspoon Tabasco

1 cup fresh bread crumbs, divided

2 cups mayonnaise

Sauté bell pepper and onion in butter for a few minutes; do not brown. Mix crab, parsley, eggs, mustard, lemon juice, Worcestershire, Tabasco, 1/2 cup bread crumbs, and mayonnaise. Do not break up crab more than necessary but do remove any shell or cartilage. Put in a 2- to 3-inch-deep casserole. Sprinkle remaining 1/2 cup of bread crumbs on the top.

Bake in a 350-degree oven until brown and hot, about 20 minutes. Serves 8 to 10.

SIDE DISHES

Mahlshooshay
Cold Lentil Salad Vinaigrette
Cervelas with Lentils
Denise's Favorite Gnocchi
Artichoke and Truffle Salad
Fried Okra
Champagne Risotto
Salade Composée
Gratin of Macaroni and Cauliflower

GEORGE ABBOTT

George Abbott is a retired businessman of a certain age who credits his vim and vigor to this dish, an old Lebanese recipe which his mother made when he was young. For many years, he has eaten a bit of it every day.

Mahlshooshay

Cook escarole and chicory together until tender. Salt to taste. Cook collard greens until tender. Salt to taste. Cook spinach until done. Salt to taste.

Drain all greens separately until they are as dry as possible. Boil black-eyed peas in 1 quart of water until tender. Do not overcook. Salt to taste. Drain and set aside.

Boil lightly salted coarse wheat according to package directions, until tender but firm. Drain and set aside in a colander until dry. It is very important that the wheat not be overcooked and that it be as dry as possible.

Sauté chopped onions in a large cast-iron skillet in 4 tablespoons olive oil until translucent. Then mix 1/2 cup olive oil and 1 cup lemon juice into the sautéed onions.

Blend all greens into a pan. Add black-eyed peas. Add coarse wheat. Blend all items together and serve. Serves 6 to 8.

3 pounds coarsely chopped escarole and chicory
salt to taste
2 pounds coarsely chopped collard greens
3 boxes (10 ounces each) frozen chopped spinach
1 cup black-eyed peas
1 cup coarse wheat (bulgur)
1 large onion, finely chopped
1/2 cup plus 4 tablespoons pure virgin olive oil, divided
1 cup fresh lemon juice

PAT (MRS. WILLIAM, JR.) BUCKLEY

I met Pat and Bill Buckley when our sons were attending school together in Rhode Island. They are marvelous hosts—charming, intelligent people whose parties are always full of lively conversation and lots of laughter. They entertain at their apartment in New York City or at their Connecticut house, which has a relaxed, easy atmosphere. This is one of Pat's favorite salads.

Cold Lentil Salad Vinaigrette

1 pound lentils

1 pound dark sausage

6 scallions

$1/2$ bunch parsley

4 ripe tomatoes, unpeeled

2 bunches watercress

VINAIGRETTE:

$1/3$ cup red wine vinegar

$1/3$ cup safflower oil

1 teaspoon Dijon mustard

$1/3$ cup olive oil

salt and pepper

Wash lentils and soak for 2 hours, then cook in boiling water for 25 minutes—or until al dente. Let cool.

Cook sausage, then slice or chop. Chop scallions. Cut parsley flowers very finely with scissors. Chop tomatoes. Mix all ingredients and refrigerate. When very cold, mound on a serving plate and surround with watercress. Pour vinaigrette (see recipe below) over the top. Serves 6.

VINAIGRETTE: Mix all ingredients well.

ᘒᕉ

H.R.H. PRINCESS FIRYAL

Princess Firyal was married to the brother of the King of Jordan, and she now lives in a beautiful house in London. This marvelous recipe is for a dish served at an elaborate buffet I attended at her house last year. Her tables were so memorable that I tried to copy them for a party I gave when I returned home.

Princess Firyal wrote, "To my mind, parties start with the excitement created around them, generating an atmosphere of fun and novelty. A lot of 'buzz' before the party gives an atmosphere of mystery and anticipation of merriment.

"Once I have supervised all the decoration, menus, arrangements, music, and so on, and five minutes before the first guest arrives, I say a prayer, take a deep breath, think of myself as a guest, and set about enjoying my friends' company. A hostess who appears happy at her own dinner radiates a quality that is contagious to her guests."

This is a recipe that Princess Firyal often serves at her wonderful buffets.

CERVELAS:

$1^{1}/4$ pound green lentils

1 carrot

1 large onion

2 cloves garlic

$1^{1}/2$ pounds cervelas (pork sausage, sometimes called Saucisson de Paris)

salt and pepper

3 large tablespoons French salad dressing

2 large tablespoons diced tomatoes

1 bunch fresh chives

Cervelas with Lentils

Wash and cook lentils slowly, boiling in lightly salted water, and add whole peeled carrot, onion, and garlic cloves.

Cook the cervelas separately in boiling water for 20 minutes.

Once cooked, place lentils in a dish, salt and pepper to taste, and top with warm cervelas. Coat with salad dressing and decorate with diced tomatoes and chopped chives.

DENISE (MRS. PRENTICE COBB) HALE

*D*enise is a hostess of some note, who has very definite ideas about entertaining. She insists on proper lighting, only invites people she likes, and loathes long cocktail hours. "When I have a dinner at home, the cocktail hour lasts exactly thirty-five minutes," she told me. Today, Denise lives in San Francisco, where she is known for her impeccable flair for entertaining.

Denise's Favorite Gnocchi

To make the gnocchi, heat the milk, butter, salt, and pepper in a saucepan. When the butter is melted and the mixture has come to a boil, remove from heat and add the flour all at once.

Replace the saucepan on the heat, stirring constantly with a wooden spoon. Cook until the mixture begins to sizzle and pull away from the sides of the pan. Pour out onto a dinner plate, flatten with a wooden spoon, and cover with plastic wrap placed directly on the surface. Set aside to cool.

Bring a large pan of salted water to a simmer.

When the gnocchi mixture has cooled, remove the plastic wrap and transfer the mixture to a bowl. Add the eggs, one at a time, stirring constantly with a wooden spoon. Each egg must be completely absorbed before the next is added. Add the Gruyère and season to taste with salt and pepper.

Fill a pastry bag fitted with a $^3/_4$-inch tip. Rest the metal tip on the edge of the pan of simmering water, then press the bag, twisting it from the bottom, and cut the mixture into $^1/_2$-inch pieces as it emerges, using a knife. Let the gnocchi fall into the water in batches of 30; simmer each batch for 3 or 4 minutes, then remove with a slotted spoon and drain on clean tea towels. Cook all the gnocchi this way.

To prepare the béchamel, melt butter in a saucepan. In a blender, blend together the flour, milk, salt, and pepper. Pour the mixture into the saucepan with the melted butter, then add the cream and cook, stirring, until the mixture comes to a boil. Lower the heat to medium and cook for 5 minutes, stirring constantly. Remove from the heat, then stir in the Gruyère and

CONTINUED

GNOCCHI:

1 cup plus 2 tablespoons milk

5$^1/_2$ tablespoons butter

$^1/_2$ teaspoon coarse salt

$^1/_4$ teaspoon freshly ground white pepper

1 cup all-purpose flour

4 medium eggs

3$^1/_2$ ounces ($^3/_4$ cup) Gruyère cheese, freshly grated

salt and pepper

BECHAMEL SAUCE:

1$^1/_2$ tablespoons butter

2$^1/_2$ tablespoons all-purpose flour

2 cups milk

$^1/_2$ teaspoon coarse salt

$^1/_4$ teaspoon freshly ground white pepper

$^3/_4$ cup plus 1 tablespoon cream

3 tablespoons freshly grated Gruyère

3 tablespoons freshly grated Parmesan cheese

TO FINISH THE DISH:

2 tablespoons freshly grated
  Gruyère

2 tablespoons freshly grated
  Parmesan cheese

freshly ground white pepper

ARTICHOKE AND TRUFFLE SALAD:

5 large artichokes

2 lemons

2 tablespoons extra virgin olive
  oil

3 ounces haricots verts (French
  green beans)

$1/2$ cup truffle vinaigrette (see
  recipe to follow)

1 cup frisée lettuce

$1/2$ quart bite-size pieces of mixed
  salad greens, washed and
  dried (preferably a mix of
  mâche, red and green oak leaf,
  curly endive, watercress, and
  radicchio).

$2^1/2$ ounces black truffles, thinly
  sliced

2 ounces cooked foie gras, diced

salt

GNOCCHI, continued

Parmesan. Cover with plastic wrap placed directly on the surface and set aside to cool.

Preheat the oven to 375 degrees.

Place a few tablespoons of béchamel sauce on the bottom of a shallow 3-quart glass or porcelain baking dish, and arrange gnocchi in 1 or 2 layers. Add the rest of the béchamel, pouring it evenly on top of the gnocchi. (Note: Up to this point, the dish may be prepared two days in advance.) Sprinkle with 2 tablespoons each Gruyère and Parmesan, and freshly ground white pepper. Bake for 45 minutes or until lightly browned. Serve at once. Serves 8.

❧

VERONICA (MRS. RANDOLPH) HEARST

Veronica is the beautiful wife of publisher Randolph Hearst. She is intelligent, aware, and very involved in the publishing business. The Hearsts entertain a great deal, both for business and for pleasure. Randy is a kind, gentle man who knows how to make his guests feel relaxed. And Veronica is a terrific hostess and knows food. She serves this wonderful salad with a menu of red wine cod with fried leeks, potato purée, baby carrots, and sautéed spinach.

Artichoke and Truffle Salad

PREPARE ARTICHOKE BOTTOMS:

Snap off the stem of the artichoke. Cut off and discard the bottom leaves, using a sharp knife. Continue cutting the leaves until you reach the soft inner core.

Cut off the top of the artichoke, leaving the bottom about 1 inch high. Trim the artichoke bottom to remove all the tough outer green parts so that it has a round regular shape and a smooth edge.

Rub the bottom well with the cut edge of a lemon to prevent it from discoloring and drop the artichoke bottom into a bowl of cold water.

Bring a large saucepan of salted water to a boil. Add the juice of the lemon, the oil, and the artichoke bottom, and cook at a simmer for about 20 minutes. The bottom should be tender when pierced with the point of a knife. Let cool enough to handle and remove the choke with a spoon. It should slide off easily if the artichoke is cooked enough.

Cover the bottoms with the cooking liquid and refrigerate. When ready to use, remove from liquid, halve each of the artichokes lengthwise, and slice paper thin.

PREPARE HARICOTS VERTS:

String the beans by snapping off one end and pulling down the length of the bean to remove the string.

Bring a saucepan of salted water to a boil. Add the beans and cook until crisp-tender, 3 to 5 minutes. Drain and refresh under cold water, then drain again. Cut into 2-inch lengths.

PREPARE TRUFFLE VINAIGRETTE:

In a small bowl, whisk together the mustard, shallots, and vinegars. Add the oils in a thin stream, whisking until well blended. Season with salt and pepper to taste. Add minced black truffle. Store tightly covered in refrigerator for up to 1 week. Be sure to shake the jar vigorously to re-blend the ingredients. Makes approximately $1^1/_3$ cups.

PREPARE SALAD:

In a large salad bowl, combine the frisée lettuce, salad greens, and haricots verts, and toss with your hands. Add the thinly sliced truffle and diced foie gras and toss again.

Pour the vinaigrette over the salad and toss gently and thoroughly until all items are lightly covered but evenly coated. They shouldn't swim in the dressing.

Mound the greens in the center of each serving plate and cover the mounds completely with the sliced artichokes, overlapping the slices to form a little mountain. Sprinkle more of the vinaigrette over all. Serve immediately. Serves 4.

TRUFFLE VINAIGRETTE:
$^1/_2$ teaspoon Dijon mustard
$^1/_2$ teaspoon finely chopped shallots
2 tablespoons champagne vinegar
2 tablespoons sherry vinegar
$^1/_2$ cup extra virgin olive oil
$^1/_2$ cup canola oil
2 tablespoons truffle oil
2 tablespoons minced black truffle
salt
freshly ground white pepper

ॐ

MARIANNE ROGERS

There is a warmth and ease to Southern entertaining that you can't find anywhere else. Marianne typifies this style. She told me that when she was married to country singer Kenny Rogers, "On several occasions we had a gathering of a few couples and we'd all cook the meal for the evening in our kitchen. Kenny would cook carrot cake from scratch and I would roast a leg of lamb. Another couple would make the vegetables, another the salad, and so on. It would always be a lot of fun because of the mistakes we made, and quite surprisingly, the food was delicious."

Several years ago when my daughter Lisa and I were on a tour of the South, we spent a night at the Rogers farm in Athens, Georgia. Their helicopter picked us up at the airport and transported us to the farm where we enjoyed a casual, old-fashioned Southern dinner. Marianne's favorite Southern recipe is Fried Okra. There are many variations, but hers is the one her mother used when she was a child.

Fried Okra

fresh okra
salt and pepper
cornmeal to coat
$1/3$ cup vegetable oil

Wash fresh okra in cold water and lay on towel to absorb the moisture. Cut off the ends and slice into $1/2$-inch pieces. Salt and pepper to taste.

Pour cornmeal over okra until it is completely coated. Now it is ready to fry.

Using a cast-iron skillet, heat vegetable oil until it is hot enough to fry, then reduce heat to medium. Cook okra until it is brown on one side, then turn over and brown the other side. Do not overcook. When it is golden brown, remove okra from the heat. Serve warm.

&

YVETTE (MRS. HOWARD) RUBY

Yvette Ruby is well known as the film star Yvette Mimeuex. She has retired from acting and lives with her husband Howard in Los Angeles and Paris.

Yvette told me, "We love to give cozy dinners for ten or twelve people. Occasionally we give a madcap party, featuring some kind of dancing and a show—flamenco, tango, even lambada!

"We serve a great deal of Italian food. Not the red sauce restaurant kind, but a homestyle treatment of meats, vegetables, and fruits. Most dinners we give include a pasta or risotto. This one is simple to make."

Champagne Risotto

Brown the onion in the olive oil and butter until golden. Add the rice and cook for 3 minutes. Add 2 cups champagne and keep stirring. As the champagne evaporates, add small amounts of boiling water and the bouillon cubes. Continue cooking for 15 minutes, still stirring and adding water in small amounts.

Before serving, stir in the grated Parmesan cheese. Shake the champagne bottle a few times to make it fizz, then pour the fizz over the rice. Serves 4.

RISOTTO:
1/2 onion, chopped
1 tablespoon olive oil
1 tablespoon butter
8 handfuls rice
1 bottle of champagne
1 cube chicken bouillon
1 cube beef bouillon
2 tablespoons freshly grated
    Parmesan chees

SAO SCHLUMBERGER

Sao, the widow of Pierre Schlumberger, a Paris and Houston businessman, is known for her simple and original dinners. Today, Sao lives in a contemporary apartment near the Eiffel Tower in Paris, France.

Sao's philosophy of entertaining is this: "A big smile, great wines, and interesting conversation makes a party." This simple salad is remarkably good.

Salade Composée

Chop and mix all ingredients and cover with vinaigrette dressing.

SALADE COMPOSEE:
1/4 pound string beans, cooked
1 apple
1 avocado, diced
2 diced artichoke hearts
handful of chopped nuts
3 quail eggs, hard-cooked
vinaigrette

CATHERINE (MRS. BASIL) ZOULLAS

Catie, a lovely Greek friend who entertains in Athens and New York, gave me this recipe.

Gratin of Macaroni and Cauliflower

Trim the head of cauliflower and plunge it for 5 minutes in salted boiling water. Cool under cold, running water, then drain and separate into florets. Cook the pasta in boiling salted water until done but firm. Cool under cold water. CONTINUED

MACARONI AND CAULIFLOWER:
1 head cauliflower
1 pound macaroni
1 tablespoon chopped onion
1 tablespoon butter
1 teaspoon flour
2 cups milk
2 cups heavy cream
1 cup mascarpone cheese
1/4 tablespoon grated or
    powdered nutmeg
salt and pepper
6 ounces cooked ham, cut in
    thick slices
2 ounces grated Parmesan
    cheese (2/3 cup)
3 ounces grated Emmenthal
    cheese (3/4 cup)

Cook the onion in the butter over medium heat. Add the flour, then the milk, cream, mascarpone, and nutmeg. Bring to a boil, stirring with a spoon. Reduce heat and simmer for 3 to 5 minutes while stirring. Add salt and pepper to taste.

Butter the bottom of a gratin dish, then place a layer of ham, pasta, and cauliflower along the bottom. Cover with some sauce, then add a second layer and cover with the rest of the sauce. Sprinkle with Parmesan and Emmenthal cheese and bake at 375 degrees for 30 minutes. If the cheese has not browned, just before serving, flash it under the broiler to achieve a nice golden color. Serves 4 to 6.

DESSERTS AND PASTRIES

Marble Bavarian Soufflé
Chocolate Bedford Cake
Blu' Bana Bread
Dan's Double Chocolate Chip Cookies
Grand Marnier Mousse Luers
Simnel Cakes
Peanut Butter Ice Cream
Caramelized Apples

HARRIET (MRS. ARMAND) DEUTSCH

The Deutschs are popular hosts and entertain with an eclectic mix of guests from the entertainment, political, and business worlds. Harriet's Marble Bavarian Soufflé is a favorite, and I'm delighted she has shared it with me.

Marble Bavarian Soufflé

BAVARIAN SOUFFLE:

3 envelopes ($^{1}/_{4}$ ounce each) unflavored gelatin
1 cup cold water
8 eggs, separated
1 cup sugar, divided
1 tablespoon vanilla
$^{1}/_{4}$ cup all-purpose flour
1 quart milk
4 ounces (4 squares) semisweet chocolate
4 tablespoons unsweetened cocoa
6 drops yellow food color
$^{1}/_{4}$ teaspoon salt
1 cup heavy cream, whipped

On the day before or early in the day, sprinkle gelatin over cold water to soften. In a large saucepan, combine egg yolks with $^{3}/_{4}$ cup of sugar and the vanilla. Blend in the flour and stir until the mixture is smooth. Add milk, blending well. Cook over low-to-medium heat, stirring constantly until custard coats the back of the spoon, then remove from heat.

Add gelatin mixture and stir to completely dissolve. Refrigerate, stirring occasionally, until a small amount mounds when dropped from a spoon.

At the same time, fold a 35 x 12-inch piece of aluminum foil in half lengthwise; wrap around the outside of a china soufflé dish which measures 10 inches to the brim, so a collar 3 inches high stands above the rim. Fasten it with cellophane tape.

Melt semisweet chocolate in a small saucepan set over hot, not boiling, water.

Divide cooled custard mixture in half, placing each half in a separate large bowl. Into one half stir melted semisweet chocolate and cocoa until mixture is smooth. Into the other half, stir yellow food coloring.

Whip the cream. Beat egg whites with salt until they form soft peaks, then gradually add ¼ cup of sugar while beating until stiff. Fold half of the whipped cream and half of the beaten egg whites into the chocolate mixture. Into the yellow mixture, fold the remaining cream and egg whites.

Into the soufflé dish, alternately spoon the yellow and chocolate mixtures. Then, with a rubber scraper, cut through the mixture several times, swirling light and dark batters into a marbleized effect.

Refrigerate several hours or overnight. Before serving, remove the foil. Serve with medium-thick chocolate sauce. Serves 16.

**See Egg Caution note in the appendix, page 188.

🐌

NICOLE, DUCHESS OF BEDFORD

*B*edford Chocolate Cake is their traditional family birthday cake. It is very rich, but worth the added calories.

Bedford Chocolate Cake

Preheat oven to 375 degrees.

Melt instant coffee in a little water. In a saucepan, melt chocolate and butter on low heat. Add coffee and grated lemon zest. Mix well and remove from heat.

Beat egg yolks with sugar until creamy. Beat egg whites until very firm.

CONTINUED

1 tablespoon instant coffee

9 ounces dark cooking chocolate

3½ ounces (7 tablespoons) butter

zest from 1 lemon

4 eggs, separated

3½ ounces (7 tablespoons) sugar

1¾ ounces (7 tablespoons) flour

3½ ounces (⅔ cup) cornstarch

Add flour and cornstarch to chocolate mixture. Add egg yolks to chocolate mixture. Fold in beaten egg whites.

Pour mixture into a medium-size mold well coated with butter. Bake for 18 minutes. Remove from oven and turn over a rack to cool.

ICING:

Melt sugar, butter, and chocolate in a saucepan. Stir well until completely melted. Add milk and simmer over low heat for a few minutes. Pour hot icing over the cake and decorate with walnuts.

ICING:

3 cups sugar

1/2 pound (2 sticks) butter

4 ounces (4 squares) dark chocolate

4 ounces (1/2 cup) milk

walnuts

ભ

BETTY (MRS. GERALD) FORD

Betty Ford's warmth and down-to-earth style make her a favorite hostess. She told me that she and President Ford entertain less frequently these days, due to his busy schedule and her work at the Betty Ford Clinic. But when they do, they always have the most interesting mix of guests. "President Ford and I have been fortunate in having the opportunity to entertain some of the most interesting and nicest people from around the world," she says.

These days, they prefer casual gatherings at their house in Beaver Creek, Colorado. "The mood and the pace are just a bit more relaxed in those beautiful mountains," Betty told me. "Perhaps my favorite event is a buffet dinner of several tables held during the World Forum in June. I like to begin with the first course presented by being served. Then everyone gets up and mingles and converses as they go to the buffet. The guests at this dinner are mainly political and business leaders from all over the world. They bring new concepts, interesting ideas, and wonderful stories to our dinner table. The conversation is so lively that the guests tend to linger well into the night. We treasure the insights and friendships that have been shared."

Betty likes to include her favorite family bread and cookies on the table. They were created by Dan, a cook who has been with the family for many years.

Blu' Bana Bread

Preheat oven to 325 degrees.

Grease and flour 2 loaf pans.

Cream together butter and sugar. Beat in eggs and add vanilla. Fold in mashed bananas and 2 cups of the flour. Place 2 remaining cups of flour, less 2 tablespoons, in a sifter and add allspice, baking soda, baking powder, and salt. Sift and fold into mixture.

Sprinkle blueberries with remaining 2 tablespoons flour, coat well, and fold into batter.

Divide batter between 2 loaf pans. Bake for approximately 50 minutes. Test with a toothpick to determine doneness.

BANANA BREAD:

$1/2$ pound (2 sticks) butter

2 cups sugar

4 eggs

2 teaspoons vanilla

5 ripe bananas, mashed

4 cups sifted flour, divided

3 teaspoons allspice

2 teaspoons baking soda

1 teaspoon baking powder

$1/2$ teaspoon salt

2 cups frozen or fresh blueberries, drained

Dan's Double Chocolate Chip Cookies

Preheat oven to 350 degrees.

Beat the butter and sugar together until light and fluffy. Beat in the eggs, one at a time. Beat in the vanilla or brandy. Melt the unsweetened chocolate in a dish over hot water. Stir the melted chocolate and sour cream into the creamed mixture.

Sift together the flour, cocoa, baking soda, baking powder, and salt. Stir the dry ingredients gradually into the melted chocolate mixture to form a batter. Stir in the white chocolate chips and nuts.

Drop the batter by tablespoons onto an ungreased cookie sheet. Bake for 10 minutes.

Makes about 5 dozen.

CHOCOLATE CHIP COOKIES:

$1/2$ pound (2 sticks) butter

$1^3/4$ cups sugar

2 eggs

2 teaspoons vanilla or brandy

1 ounce unsweetened baking chocolate

$1/4$ cup sour cream

2 cups unbleached all-purpose flour

$3/4$ cup unsweetened cocoa

$1/2$ teaspoon baking soda

$1/4$ teaspoon baking powder

$1/2$ teaspoon salt

12 ounces (2 cups) white chocolate chips, chopped

1 cup shelled, chopped Brazil nuts or almonds

WENDY (MRS. WILLIAM) LUERS

During the Reagan administration, William Luers was American Ambassador to Czechoslovakia. In 1985, I visited the Luers and I can still remember stepping down off the plane and feeling as though I had stepped into another world. The Iron Curtain still existed, and guards with dogs were lined along the top of the stairs, looking quite ominous. But then Wendy appeared behind them, smiling and waving, welcoming us with great warmth.

This dessert was served at the Embassy. I loved it so much I persuaded Wendy to give me the recipe.

Grand Marnier Mousse Luers

4 eggs, separated, plus 2 additional egg yolks, at room temperature

¹⁄₂ cup sugar

1 envelope (¹⁄₄ ounce) unflavored gelatin

¹⁄₂ cup Grand Marnier

zest of orange, grated

1 cup heavy cream

¹⁄₂ teaspoon cream of tartar

strawberries for garnish

Separate eggs into 2 bowls. Combine sugar and gelatin and add them to the egg yolks. Beat until pale yellow and thick. Heat on top of a double boiler until gelatin and sugar have dissolved. Do not simmer or boil as eggs will curdle.

Stir in Grand Marnier and orange zest, and cook for 1 minute. Do not overheat or liquor will evaporate. Cool completely.

Beat cream stiff. With a large rubber spatula, fold cream into cooled custard base. Beat egg whites with cream of tartar to soft peaks. Fold one third of whites into mousse, then add the rest.

Pour into a 6-cup soufflé dish, cover with plastic wrap, and refrigerate 4 to 6 hours or overnight. Decorate with strawberries to serve. Serves 12.

**See Egg Caution note in the appendix, page 188.

ISABEL (MRS. GARRET) LEAHEY JR.

Isabel, the mother of three, is a young friend of my children. She is a talented and energetic entertainer who does all the cooking herself. Every Christmas, Isabel sends this cake as a gift to friends.

She explained to me, "Simnel is a rich currant cake eaten on a Sunday in the middle of Lent in some parts of England. This recipe dates back to 1648. I added the almond paste to make the flavor richer."

Simnel Cakes

SIMNEL CAKES:

³⁄₄ pound (3 sticks) butter

2 cups sugar

6 eggs

2¹⁄₂ cups flour

¹⁄₂ cup citrus peel (lemon and/or orange)

1 box (15 ounces) golden raisins

1 box (10 ounces) currants

1 to 1¹⁄₂ cups canned almond filling

almond paste

Preheat oven to 350 degrees.

Cream butter. Add sugar and beat until light. Add eggs. Continue beating until incorporated. Add flour. Mix thoroughly, then add citrus peel, raisins, and currants.

Using miniature muffin tins with liners, add 1 teaspoon of batter to each cup, then 1 teaspoon of almond filling, then about ¼ teaspoon of almond paste. Top with an additional teaspoon of batter. Bake for 15 to 20 minutes and cool on a rack. Makes 60 to 80.

CHARDEE (MRS. T.W.) TRAINER

*C*hardee has become famous among her friends for this recipe. It is so good that when I am invited to her house in Beverly Hills, I always hope she'll serve it.

Peanut Butter Ice Cream

Mix half-and-half and peanut butter in a saucepan and heat slowly to scalding. Remove from heat and add the sugar slowly, stirring to dissolve. Cool. Then add vanilla and chill. When mixture is thoroughly chilled, place in an ice cream maker and mix for 20 to 30 minutes. Makes about 2 quarts.

1 quart half-and-half
1 cup peanut butter
1 cup sugar
2 teaspoons vanilla
(for richer ice cream, substitute 1 cup heavy cream for 1 cup half-and-half)

CONNIE WALD

*C*onnie admitted, "I stole this from my friend Audrey Hepburn, who was a superb cook."

Caramelized Apples

Peel, core, and slice the apples, and place in a bowl of cold water.

In a copper pan, caramelize 1 cup of sugar. When done, toss in the apples and cover. Cook over a medium heat for approximately 8 to 10 minutes, stirring occasionally until it draws its own juices.

Add remaining 2 cups of sugar, lemon juice, and cinnamon. Cover and cook slowly, stirring occasionally, until it reaches a dark, rich color. Refrigerate. Serve chilled with a dollop of crème fraîche. Serves 8.

8 Granny Smith apples
3 cups sugar, divided
1 tablespoon lemon juice
1 teaspoon ground cinnamon
crème fraîche (see appendix, p.188)

CHAPTER SEVEN

Famous Dishes From Great Restaurants

TOP CHEFS SHARE THEIR SECRETS

Entertaining in restaurants has become a way of life in this busy day and age. But it needn't be an impersonal experience. The restaurants I most enjoy are those with a warm and inviting ambience, where the food and service are very good. When I am hosting a dinner in a restaurant, I often invite guests to my house first for drinks and appetizers, and we go to the restaurant from there. This adds an extra personal touch, since inviting people to your house is always a friendly thing to do. The restaurants in this chapter are among my favorites. The chefs have graciously shared some of their most popular recipes. Most of them have never been published before, which makes it possible for you to serve something unique. Even though you might live hundreds or thousands of miles away from any of these well-known restaurants, you can capture the experience of being there.

The Bistro Garden

BEVERLY HILLS, CALIFORNIA

The Bistro Garden is one of the prettiest restaurants in Beverly Hills, and it's a great place for people watching. The owner, Kurt Nicholas, was maitre d' at Romanoff's, the famous restaurant in Beverly Hills (no longer in existence) where Alfred

CHICKEN QUESADILLA:

$1/4$ onion, sliced

$1/2$ chicken breast, cooked and
    julienned

pinch of salt and pepper

2 ounces brown sauce

2 slices Monterey jack cheese

whole green chili, sliced

1 flour tortilla

sour cream and cherry peppers for
    garnish

GUACAMOLE:

1 avocado, mashed plus shells for
    serving

1 teaspoon diced onion

1 Italian tomato, peeled and diced

$1/3$ bunch fresh cilantro, chopped

1 jalapeño pepper, chopped
    (see note)

salt

white pepper

SALSA:

5 Italian tomatoes, poached,
    skinned, and diced

2 jalapeño peppers, diced

1 bunch cilantro, chopped

salt

white pepper

squeeze of lemon

SEA BASS:

1 sea bass ($3^1/2$ pounds)

salt and pepper

fresh herbs (parsley, tarragon,
    chervil, basil)

$5^1/2$ cups flour

4 cups salt

1 tablespoon herbes de provence

2 tablespoons olive oil

1 cup water

and I met. He first opened The Bistro, patterning it after a restaurant in Paris. This was followed by The Bistro Garden, which has become a local favorite. The Chicken Quesadilla is one of the most popular dishes.

Chicken Quesadilla

Sauté onions, then add chicken and a pinch of salt and pepper. Combine with 2 ounces of brown sauce. Place cheese, chili, and chicken mixture on one half of the tortilla and fold to enclose.

Add sour cream and cherry peppers as a garnish and serve with guacamole and salsa. Serves 1.

GUACAMOLE:

Mix all ingredients and serve in half avocado shells.

SALSA:

Mix ingredients and serve.

Note: When preparing fresh chilies, wear rubber gloves for protection against oils that later can cause a burning sensation on skin.

Hotel Bel Air
SAINT-JEAN-CAP-FERRAT, FRANCE

While I was staying at the beautiful Hotel Bel Air, the great chef Jean Claude Guillon prepared this wonderful sea bass for me.

Sea Bass in Salt Crust Pastry

Preheat oven to 500 degrees.

Empty, clean, and scale the bass. Dry well. Season the inside with salt and pepper and stuff with fresh herbs.

Prepare the salt crust by mixing the flour, 4 cups salt, herbes de provence, olive oil, and water.

The pastry should have the same consistency as short crust pastry, and can be prepared the day before. Roll out the pastry like a tart. Place the sea bass on the pastry and cover. Bake for 30 minutes, then remove. When the crust comes away, you have a delicious fish that has been steamed in the salt crust. Serves 6 to 8.

Claridge's

LONDON, ENGLAND

*C*laridge's is my favorite hotel in London. The lobby is always bustling, and tea is a must. The manager, Michael Bentley, shared two recipes which have a distinct British style and flavor.

Medallions of Wild Salmon with Leeks and Asparagus

Melt half the butter in a saucepan. Add shallots and briefly cook to soften. Add 1⅓ cups of the chicken stock and simmer gently to infuse the flavor; reduce to a syrupy liquid consistency.

With the remaining butter, cook the leeks to soften with the lid on the saucepan to create some steam. Add remaining chicken stock and simmer until leeks are thoroughly cooked.

Add a little cream to the leeks and thicken by cooking. Season to taste with salt and pepper.

Pour the remaining cream into the reduced chicken stock and simmer to flavor; thicken sufficiently to coat the back of a spoon.

Purée half the creamed leeks and add to the chicken cream sauce. Reserve the remaining leeks to serve.

Cut asparagus spears 2 inches from the tip and peel them. Blanch for 4 to 5 minutes and dip into iced water.

Blanch the remainder of the asparagus in salt water, then purée with a little of the chicken sauce into a green pulp.

Add this to the chicken sauce and briefly reboil. Strain and press the resulting pulp through the sieve. Keep the sauce warm until serving.

TO SERVE:

Quick fry with oil, grill, or steam the salmon, previously seasoned to your liking.

Arrange the creamed, braised leeks in the center of the serving dish. Place the salmon snugly on top. Surround it with leeks and asparagus sauce (willow green in color), then place warm asparagus tips around it in such a fashion as to create a pattern. Place warm, diced tomatoes between the tips in small bunches. Decorate with green leaves of parsley or chervil. Serves 4.

¼ pound (1 stick) butter, divided
1 ounce (2 tablespoons) chopped shallots (or onions)
2 cups chicken stock, divided
1 pound fresh leeks, cut into ⅛-inch rounds
2 cups heavy cream, divided
salt and pepper
12 asparagus spears
½ cup vegetable oil, for frying
4 medallions of salmon, 6 ounces each
4 tablespoons diced, peeled tomatoes
4 sprigs fresh parsley or chervil

Pot Roasted Filet of Kent Lamb
with Fresh Minted Sauce

2 pounds loin filet of lamb,
    trimmed

salt and pepper

1/2 cup peanut oil

3 1/2 ounces (7 tablespoons plus a
    nugget) butter, divided

water

2 tablespoons minced shallots,
    divided

1 cup white wine

2 1/2 cups brown, thickened lamb
    stock

1 bunch fresh mint, divided

1 1/2 cups heavy cream

new potatoes, boiled

Season the meat with salt and pepper, and allow to stand for a while to take off the chill.

Brown meat by shallow frying briefly over high heat in a mixture of oil and 7 tablespoons butter.

Add a small amount of water, add 1 tablespoon shallots, cover and simmer for 18 to 20 minutes (or to your preference), basting frequently.

Transfer meat and keep warm.

Remove excess grease in the pan and return to heat. Add 1 more tablespoon of shallots and briefly cook; do not overfry.

Pour the wine on the shallots and cook down to a syrup. (If meat trimmings are available, add to the pan.)

Add the meat stock and bring to a boil. Skim as the foam is forming. Cook at low heat to infuse, then add half the fresh mint. Reduce the sauce by a third or so, providing you obtain good mint flavor while retaining the taste of the meat. Should the mixture require thickening, do so with a little cornstarch.

Strain two thirds of the sauce and reserve.

Return the remainder of the sauce to the heat and cook to reduce by half, then add heavy cream and remaining mint leaves. Cook slowly to flavor the creamed mint sauce, and skim.

Check the seasoning, adjust accordingly, and strain the cream sauce. Add any juices from the meat.

Add a nugget of butter to the brown sauce and whisk thoroughly.

TO SERVE:

Carve the reheated meat at an angle into 1/4-inch-thick slices. Transfer to a serving dish; slightly separate the slices in a slatted fashion into a semicircle.

Surround the meat with cream sauce and pour the brown sauce over the meat to gloss it. This will produce the desired effect as it runs into the cream sauce, creating a pattern.

Garnish with new boiled potatoes and fresh sprigs of mint. Serves 8.

Granita

MALIBU, CALIFORNIA

Granita, a restaurant at the beach in Malibu, is owned by Wolfgang Puck. Granita has become a big hit in Los Angeles for food like the following dish.

Crisp Potato Galette
with Gravlax and Dill Crème Fraîche

Toss grated potatoes in one-half the clarified butter. Season with salt and freshly ground black pepper.

Heat 2 nonstick sauté pans over high heat until they're nearly smoking. Divide remaining butter between the 2 pans. Add the potatoes evenly to the pans, shaping them into thick pancakes. Cook for 1 to 2 minutes, then reduce heat. Sauté until almost golden brown. Use a spatula to check the undersides of the pancakes, turn over, and cook the other sides until they're golden. Remove them from the pan and warm in a 425-degree oven for 10 minutes.

PREPARE THE DILL CREAM:

In a bowl, mix together shallots, dill, crème fraîche or sour cream, the juice of ¹/₂ lemon, and salt and pepper to taste.

Remove potatoes from the oven while warm. Spread with dill cream and cover with slices of gravlax. Lightly brush gravlax with olive oil, then sprinkle with black pepper and the remaining lemon juice. Cut potatoes into desired portions and garnish with salmon caviar and chopped chives. Serve immediately. Serves 4 to 6.

3 potatoes, peeled and grated

¹/₂ pound (1 cup) clarified butter, divided

salt and freshly ground black pepper

3 shallots, minced

5 sprigs fresh dill, chopped

¹/₂ cup crème fraîche or sour cream

juice of 1 lemon, divided

1 pound gravlax (or smoked salmon), thinly sliced

1 tablespoon olive oil

3 ounces salmon caviar

¹/₂ bunch fresh chives, chopped

PASTA:

10¹/₂ ounces flour

2³/₄ ounces cooked, chopped
    spinach (2³/₄ cups raw)

1 ounce (³/₄ cup) arugula

3 egg yolks, room temperature

1 whole egg, room temperature

SAUCE:

1 cup plus 2 tablespoons
    béchamel sauce

2²/₃ ounces cooked prosciutto,
    chopped

pinch of mace

2¹/₂ ounces (³/₄ cup grated)
    Parmesan cheese

Harry's Bar
LONDON, ENGLAND

Harry's Bar is my favorite restaurant in London. Actually, it's a private club owned by Mark Birley. They gave me this wonderful pasta recipe.

Tagliolini Verde Gratinatti al Prosciutto

Make the pasta according to the directions for your pasta machine. Cook the pasta in plenty of boiling, salted water. Drain.

In a saucepan, mix the béchamel, prosciutto, and mace and bring to a boil. Add the hot pasta and mix well before turning the mixture into a gratin dish. Sprinkle the Parmesan over the top and place under a hot grill or broiler until brown. Serves 4.

Hotel Plaza Athéné
PARIS, FRANCE

There's nothing nicer than being served dinner on the terrace of this hotel on a warm summer evening. The Pannequets Brioches recipe is simple and delicious—a great finale for any dinner.

brioche, cut in 2¹/₂-inch rounds

1 cup plus 3 tablespoons milk

1 cup plus 3 tablespoons heavy
    cream

4 eggs

3 egg yolks

4³/₈ ounces (8 tablespoons plus 2
    teaspoons) sugar

vanilla

butter

orange marmalade, warmed

vanilla ice cream

orange slices

Pannequets Brioches

Cut a high, round brioche, which is a French bun made with eggs and butter, into slices.

Mix together the milk, cream, eggs, egg yolks, sugar, and vanilla to taste. Dip the slices of brioche into the mixture.

Melt butter in a frying pan and fry each slice of brioche. Serve on a plate, three slices per person, with 2 tablespoons of warm orange marmalade and a scoop of vanilla ice cream, and decorate with orange slices. Serves 4 to 6.

La Grenouille
NEW YORK, NEW YORK

This is a lovely New York restaurant, with classic French cuisine. It's one of the prettiest restaurants in the city, with fresh flowers and sunny decor. The owner, Monsieur Masson, supplied this simple chicken recipe, which is light and very good. I also asked for the Grand Marnier Sauce; it's wonderful with fruits and fruit tarts.

Poularde Gros Sel

Place the chickens in a large pan. Add the carrots, turnips, leeks, celery, and cabbage. Cover the chickens and vegetables with chicken stock. Bring to a boil, then skim the top. Cover and poach over low heat for about 40 minutes, until chickens are tender.

Drain the chickens and vegetables and arrange on a hot platter with the chickens in the center and the vegetables surrounding them.

Serve with Sauce Raifort and coarse salt on the side.

SAUCE RAIFORT:

In a saucepan, cook 4 tablespoons horseradish in 1 cup of cream consommé (plain consommé with 1 tablespoon of cream). Add 1 cup of cream and white bread crumbs. Bring the sauce to a boil, then strain through a cheesecloth. Add fresh, grated horseradish to taste. Stir, strain, and serve. Serves 8.

2 chickens, 3 pounds each
10 carrots, cut in small round shapes
10 small turnips, cut in small round shapes
12 leeks, white part only, cut in 3-inch pieces
2 pieces celery
1 green cabbage, cut in half
chicken stock
coarse salt

SAUCE:
4 tablespoons or more fresh, grated horseradish
1 cup consommé
2 cups plus 1 tablespoon heavy cream, divided
1 to 2 tablespoons white bread crumbs

Grand Marnier Sauce

5 egg yolks
¹/₂ cup plus 2 tablespoons sugar, divided
¹/₄ cup Grand Marnier, divided
1 cup heavy cream

Add the yolks and ¹/₂ cup of sugar to a 2-quart mixing bowl that will rest snugly on top of a slightly larger saucepan. Add about 2 inches of water to the saucepan and bring to a boil. Beat yolks vigorously with a wire whisk or portable electric beater, making sure to scrape around inside bottom of bowl with beater.

Place the mixing bowl on the saucepan (do not allow bowl to touch water) and continue beating for about 10 minutes or until yolks are quite thick and pale yellow. Remove bowl from saucepan and stir in half the Grand Marnier. Allow sauce to cool, then refrigerate until thoroughly cold.

Beat the cream with 2 tablespoons of sugar until it is almost but not quite stiff. Fold cream into sauce and stir in remaining Grand Marnier.

Serve with seasonal fresh fruits or fruit tarts. Serves 10.

Le Cirque

NEW YORK, NEW YORK

This restaurant, besides having four-star cuisine, has a history with our family. Alfred's cousin, Ellen Lehman McClusky, decorated it when it first opened. It still has the same look twenty years later. Daniel Boulud, once Chef de Cuisine, graciously provided this delicious, light Risotto Primavera, and the Crème Brulée, for which Le Cirque is famous.

Risotto Primavera

VEGETABLES:
¹/₄ cup asparagus tips
¹/₄ cup fresh peas
¹/₄ cup broccoli florets
¹/₄ cup diced zucchini
2 quarts boiling salted water
2 tablespoons olive oil
¹/₄ cup diced mushrooms for garnish
¹/₄ cup diced tomatoes for garnish
¹/₄ cup chopped fresh parsley for garnish

RICE:
1 onion, minced
3 tablespoons butter, divided
16 ounces arborio rice
1 cup white wine
6 cups chicken stock or water from cooking vegetables, divided
¹/₄ cup grated Parmesan cheese

Precook all the vegetables in 2 quarts of boiling water as follows: Cook the asparagus for 2 minutes, then remove to a bowl of ice water and set aside. In the same water, repeat the process for all the vegetables except the mushrooms and tomatoes. Drain.

To cook the rice: In a 2-quart casserole, melt over low heat 1 tablespoon of butter and sweat the minced onion until soft but not brown 4 to 5 minutes. Add all the rice and continue stirring with the onion for 1 to 2 minutes, being careful that the rice doesn t stick. Raise the heat to medium and add 1 cup of white wine and cook until the wine is completely reduced. At this point, add 1 cup of chicken broth or vegetable water. As the rice cooks, it will keep absorbing liquid. Continue adding liquid a little at a time so that it is always just above the rice. When the rice is almost cooked (about 15 minutes), add all the vegetables except the tomatoes and mushrooms, and continue cooking until the rice is al dente (firm on the outside but soft inside). Remove from the heat and add remaining 2 tablespoons of butter and the Parmesan cheese. Sauté the tomatoes and mushrooms in a small pan with a tablespoon of oil. Garnish the risotto with parsley and the sautéed tomatoes and mushrooms. Serves 8.

Crème Brulée

Heat heavy cream to the boiling point and add vanilla bean. Mix granulated sugar and egg yolks in a large bowl. Add hot cream and mix well. Strain into a 1½-quart mold. Cook at 250 degrees in a bain-marie (water bath) for 1 hour or until set.

Let cool and refrigerate. Before serving, sieve brown sugar and spread over crème brulée. Glaze under the broiler until it is melted and brown. Serves 8 to 10.

1 quart heavy cream
1 vanilla bean
5 ounces (½ cup plus 3 tablespoons) granulated sugar
8 egg yolks
4 ounces (½ cup plus 1⅓ tablespoons) brown sugar

L' Orangerie Restaurant

LOS ANGELES, CALIFORNIA

L' Orangerie, often called the most beautiful restaurant in Los Angeles, was opened by Virginia and Gerald Ferry as the first authentically French restaurant in L.A. The snapper and apple tart are typical of the good food served there. It's one of the restaurants to which I enjoy taking out-of-town guests.

FISH:

1 snapper, 2 pounds
1 pound Idaho potatoes
1 medium onion
1 medium leek
1 tomato
1 carrot
5 cloves garlic
thyme
1 bay leaf
1¼ cups fish stock
¼ cup dry white wine
salt and pepper
5 basil leaves, chopped

Daurade Provençale Cuite au Four

Preheat oven to 400 degrees.

Place fish in baking dish. Peel and clean all the vegetables. Slice potatoes, onions, leek, tomato, carrot, and garlic very finely. Add thyme, bay leaf, fish stock, and wine to the cooking pot and add salt and pepper to taste.

Cook all the ingredients for 10 minutes and transfer them to a baking dish with the snapper.

Bake for 25 minutes. Check from time to time and baste the fish with the juice.

Add the chopped basil leaves at the last minute of baking, and serve on the table in the baking dish. Serves 4 to 6.

APPLE TART:

4 ounces puff pastry dough
Golden Delicious apples
apple purée
melted butter
sugar
whipped cream

Apple Tart

Spread flour on the table and roll the pastry dough out until it's very thin. Place a plate (approximately 6 inches) upside down on top of dough and cut a disk. Place the disk on a cookie sheet and spread a little apple purée on top.

Peel and cut the apples in half, then slice them very thin. Arrange the slices on top of the dough, following the circular side.

Brush the apples with melted butter, then sprinkle them with sugar.

Bake at 350 degrees for 20 minutes. Serve hot with whipped cream on the side. Serves 2.

BAKED APPLES:

6 medium-sized Rome Beauty
   apples
3 tablespoons raisins
1 cinnamon stick
½ cup sugar
½ cup orange juice
1 cup apple juice
2 tablespoons butter
heavy cream
1½ ounces Grand Marnier

Mortimer's

NEW YORK, NEW YORK

Glenn Bernbaum, who is the *patron* of this popular New York restaurant, is everyone's friend. If I'm desperate, Glenn will happily give me a recipe over the phone.

Raisin-Stuffed Baked Apples

Preheat oven to 400 degrees.
Core apples about two-thirds of the way down, leaving the

bottom intact. Remove about 1 inch of peel from around the stem end. Stuff apple cavities with raisins.

In a small saucepan, combine cinnamon stick, sugar, orange juice, apple juice, and butter, and bring to a boil. Reduce heat and cook until sugar is dissolved.

Place apples in a baking pan and pour syrup over. Bake for 1½ hours. Baste frequently with syrup.

Transfer baked apples to serving dish and spoon sauce over each. Serve with heavy cream. Serves 6.

SAUCE FOR BAKED APPLES:

Mix sugar, water, liqueur, and spices. Bring to a boil and whisk in butter.

BAKED APPLE SAUCE:

4 ounces dark brown sugar

1 tablespoon water

1 tablespoon Grand Marnier

½ cinnamon stick

1 slice orange zest

4 ounces sweet butter

Matteo's
LOS ANGELES, CALIFORNIA

This is everyone's Sunday night favorite. There's always a mixed crowd, and owner Mattie Jordan is there to make sure people have a good time. His wife Jacquelin is famous for her meat loaf, which is the best I've ever tasted.

Meat Loaf Jacquelin

In a large mixing bowl, mix all ingredients well. Shape into a loaf and place in a shallow baking dish. Pour reserved tomato juice over entire loaf and sprinkle with Parmesan cheese. Garnish top with sprigs of parsley.

Bake at 350 degrees for about 1 hour and 15 minutes. Meat should be completely done and not show any pink.

Serve with mashed potatoes and Marsala Sauce.

MARSALA SAUCE:

Sauté shallots in 2 tablespoons of butter for 5 minutes. Add remaining butter and flour, stirring well. Cook 1 minute. Add beef stock and bring to a boil. Add wine and simmer 5 minutes longer.

MEAT LOAF:

2 pounds ground beef

2 slices bread moistened with water

2 medium carrots (grated or finely chopped)

1 extra large egg, or 2 small eggs

4 tablespoons fresh parsley, finely chopped

2 tablespoons onion, finely chopped

¾ cup grated Parmesan cheese

1 can (16 ounces) unseasoned tomatoes , reserve liquid

¼ teaspoon finely ground black pepper

salt (but remember Parmesan is salty)

SAUCE:

1 tablespoons shallots, finely minced

3 tablespoons butter, divided

2 tablespoons flour

1¼ cups beef stock

¼ cup Marsala wine

Spago

LOS ANGELES, CALIFORNIA

Many people would agree that Spago is in a class by itself. Wolfgang Puck was the creative genius behind what is now known as "California cuisine"—simple, fresh foods using light sauces. The Chicken Salad Vinaigrette is a perfect example.

Chicken Salad Vinaigrette

VINAIGRETTE:

1 cup orange juice

1 ounce (2 tablespoons) curry powder

3 tablespoons balsamic vinegar

2 shallots, chopped fine

salt and pepper

SALAD:

3 tablespoons olive oil

1 chicken, about 3½ pounds, boned and cut into bite-size pieces

salt and pepper

1 napa (Chinese) cabbage

1 radicchio

4 ounces Chino greens (watercress)

1 package Kaiware (thinly sliced packaged onions)

1 red bell pepper and 1 yellow bell pepper, cored, seeded, and cut into julienne

1 papaya, peeled, seeded, and cut into cubes

2 Chino or other large tomatoes, trimmed and sliced

MAKE THE VINAIGRETTE:

In a small saucepan, bring the orange juice to a boil and cook until syrupy. Set aside. In a small skillet, over moderate heat, toast the curry powder. Set aside to cool and then stir in the orange juice. Whisk in the vinegar, shallots, and salt and pepper to taste. Set aside.

MAKE THE SALAD:

Heat the olive oil in a wok or sauté pan. Sauté the chicken, stirring to cook all sides. While the chicken is cooking, season lightly with salt and pepper. Set aside to cool.

Break apart the cabbage and radicchio leaves, rinse, and then dry thoroughly. Transfer to a large mixing bowl. Add all the remaining salad ingredients except the tomatoes and toss to combine. Pour enough of the vinaigrette over the salad to coat the ingredients and again toss to combine. Adjust seasoning to taste.

TO SERVE:

Arrange a few slices of tomatoes on each plate. Divide the salad and place atop the tomatoes. Serve immediately. Serves 4.

☙

The following recipe is one of many I learned from the cooking classes I took at Spago. Francois Kwaku-Dongo, the main chef, is a talented man from the Ivory Coast of Africa. Because I ran right home from the class and tried the recipe in my own kitchen, I now make perfect risotto.

Francois's Seafood Risotto with Ginger

MAKE THE SHRIMP STOCK:

In a large saucepan or a stockpot, heat ⅓ cup oil. Add shrimp shells, onion, carrot, celery, ginger, and tomatoes, and sweat until the onion is translucent. Deglaze with the wine and cook until most of the liquid has evaporated. Cover with water or chicken stock and bring to a boil. Skim and let simmer for about 30 minutes. Strain and keep warm.

MAKE THE RISOTTO:

In a saucepan, heat ⅓ cup oil. Sweat the onion until translucent. Add the rice and coat well, stirring with a wooden spoon. Deglaze with the wine and when the wine has evaporated, add 3 cups of the stock. Stirring constantly, cook the rice until all the liquid has been absorbed. Add 3 more cups of stock and continue to cook the rice, constantly stirring, and adding more stock if necessary.

Meanwhile, in a large skillet, heat 2 tablespoons of olive oil. Sauté the shrimp, scallops, and minced garlic for 2 minutes. Stir into the rice when the rice is almost cooked and cook for 5 minutes. At this point the rice should be firm to the bite (al dente). Remove from the heat and beat in the butter, Parmesan cheese, parsley, and tomato. Serve immediately, dividing the rice and the seafood evenly. Serves 4.

SHRIMP STOCK:

⅓ cup corn or peanut oil

10 ounces shrimp, peeled, reserve shells and meat

1 medium onion, chopped

1 medium carrot, peeled and coarsely chopped

1 celery stalk, cut into pieces

4 ounces fresh ginger, peeled and chopped

3 Roma tomatoes, peeled and diced

1 cup dry white wine

water or chicken stock

RISOTTO:

⅓ cup corn or peanut oil

1 medium onion, minced

2 cups arborio rice

1 cup dry white wine

2 tablespoons olive oil

10 ounces scallops (remove the small white rounded protuberances on the sides)

3 or 4 garlic cloves, minced

¼ pound (1 stick) unsalted butter

½ cup grated Parmesan cheese (optional)

4 ounces Italian parsley, leaves only, chopped

1 Roma tomato, chopped

"21"
NEW YORK, NEW YORK

"21" is a New York classic, serving simple, excellent food. Their rice pudding is the best anywhere, and I'm delighted to have this recipe to share with you.

Rice Pudding

1 quart milk
1 pint heavy cream
$^1/_2$ teaspoon salt
1 vanilla bean
1 cup sugar, divided
$^3/_4$ cup rice, uncooked
1 egg yolk
1$^1/_2$ cups cream, whipped

In a heavy saucepan, combine milk, cream, salt, vanilla bean, and $^3/_4$ cup of sugar. Bring to a boil. Stir well, add the rice, and allow the mixture to simmer gently, covered, for 1$^3/_4$ hours on a very low heat until the rice is soft. Remove from heat and cool slightly. Blending well, stir in remaining $^1/_4$ cup of sugar and the egg yolk. Allow to cool a bit more.

Preheat broiler. Stir in all but 2 tablespoons of the whipped cream and pour mixture into a soufflé dish. (If desired, raisins may be placed on the bottom of the dish.) Make sure the mixture is cool, then spread the remaining whipped cream in a thin layer over the top. Place under the broiler—not too close—until pudding is lightly browned. Chill before serving. Serves 10 to 12.

Glorious Foods (caterer)
NEW YORK, NEW YORK

According to my New York friends, and in my own experience, Glorious Foods is a reliable, always excellent caterer. They cater everthing from dinners for two to banquets for several hundred. The Pumpkin Mousse is a classic, a favorite of even those who don't like pumpkin.

Pumpkin Mousse with Crystallized Ginger

In a small bowl, combine rum and gelatin. Stand bowl in a pan of simmering water, stirring occasionally until gelatin is completely dissolved. In the meantime, beat egg yolks and sugar until very thick.

In a bowl, combine pumpkin, cinnamon, ginger, mace, and cloves. Mix in the gelatin well and then fold in the yolk and sugar mixture. Whip the egg whites until very firm. Fold egg whites into the pumpkin mixture. Repeat with whipped cream. Pour mousse in a bowl or a hollowed-out pumpkin and let cool for at least 5 hours before serving.

Decorate top with whipped cream and sprinkle with julienne of crystallized ginger. Serves 10.

See **Egg Caution note in the appendix, page 188.

½ cup dark rum
1 envelope (¼ ounce) unflavored gelatin
6 egg yolks
4 egg whites
1 cup sugar
1½ cups pumpkin purée
¾ teaspoon ground cinnamon
¾ teaspoon ground ginger
½ teaspoon ground mace
¼ teaspoon ground cloves
1½ cups heavy cream, whipped
crystallized ginger

Restaurant du Moulin de Mougins
MOUGINS, FRANCE

When I was visiting in the South of France this summer, I had the opportunity to meet the famous chef, Roger Vergé. His four-star restaurant, Moulin de Mougins, sits high above Monte Carlo. He is not only an innovative cook, but also a charming gentleman. With his snow-white hair and mustache to match, he is very handsome; and when he offered to give me a recipe for my cookbook, I was totally enchanted! I tasted this recipe when he served it and thought it would be too difficult. Well, it's not: I've done it. I used a small slice of truffle; his way is very extravagant. I also used these mushrooms to stuff a chicken breast instead of zucchini flowers and that's also a terrific dish. The secret is in the reduction of the sauce. Of course, the truffle juice gives a special flavor, but it's also good without it.

Stuffed Zucchini Flowers
with Truffles and Mushroom Butter

STUFFING:

1 slice of soft bread

4 tablespoons milk

1 breast of chicken

salt and pepper

²/₃ cup cream

1 pound fresh mushrooms

juice of ¹/₂ lemon

¹/₂ pound (2 sticks) plus 1
    tablespoon unsalted butter,
    divided

1 shallot, minced

salt and pepper

6 small black truffles, canned or
    fresh

6 zucchini flowers

¹/₂ pound fresh spinach leaves, or
    several bunches mâche (salad
    green)

3 tablespoons crème fraîche (see
    appendix, p.188)

several sprigs fresh chervil

For the stuffing, take the crust off the bread, cut the soft part in pieces, and let them soak in milk. Mince the chicken breast and add salt and pepper. Add the bread (squeezed), mix together, and progressively add the cold cream. Keep cold.

Clean the mushrooms. Rinse quickly in cold water without letting them soak. Drain. Place the mushrooms in a food processor and finely chop, without making a purée. Place in a bowl and add the lemon juice.

Put 1 tablespoon butter in a saucepan (medium sized). When it sizzles, add the shallot, then the mushrooms: season with salt and pepper and cook for 3 to 4 minutes, stirring with a wooden spatula.

Put a stainless steel sieve over a small saucepan and drain the mushrooms (if you don't have a stainless steel sieve, put a cloth on the bottom of the sieve to prevent the mushrooms from getting black).

Reserve the juice. Place in bowl.

Add half the poultry stuffing and mushrooms.

Drain the truffles and keep the juice in the saucepan containing the mushroom juice.

Gently pat any moisture from the petals of the zucchini flowers. (Pass under water only if really necessary). Carefully open out the petals of each blossom and fill the center with ¹/₂ tablespoon of the mushroom mixture. Nestle a truffle in the center of each blossom, add some poultry stuffing and carefully close the petals up around. Place the flowers on the top part of a couscous pot or in a steamer. Cover with aluminum foil.

Remove the stems from the spinach, wash the leaves thoroughly, and drain. Place the saucepan containing the mushroom and truffle juice over medium heat and let simmer and reduce until only 3 tablespoons of liquid remain. Add the crème frâiche.

Cut the remaining butter into small pieces and add it, a little at a time, whisking over high heat after each addition, until the butter is completely incorporated.

Season with salt and pepper and remove from the heat.

About 20 minutes before serving, fill the bottom of the

couscous pot or steamer with water and place the top part with the squash blossoms over the water.

Place over high heat and steam for about 15 minutes. The flowers will be perfectly cooked when a knife can be inserted easily.

During the cooking, reheat the sauce, if necessary. To serve, spread the spinach leaves or mâche over warmed plates. Place a zucchini blossom on each plate. Season with salt and pepper, and pour a little sauce over each.

Sprinkle each portion with chervil, if using, and serve.

Serves 6.

CHAPTER EIGHT

The Bloomingdale Family Cookbook

A COLLECTION FROM MY KITCHEN

Cooking has always been a favorite pastime in my family, and we enjoy collecting and sharing recipes. My daughter Lisa takes after my mother in that she's a natural cook. She loves buzzing around the kitchen creating new concoctions. My son Geoffrey married a girl from a cooking family, too. Polly is from the Midwest. She has brought us a whole new world of recipes to try. My son Robert didn't marry a cook. When my daughter-in-law Justine came into the family, she admitted she wasn't a cook. Over time, however, she got tired of Robert bragging about his mother's cooking. Finally, in self-defense, she took cooking classes. Now she loves to cook, and we all try her recipes.

There's something about being in the kitchen, surrounded by the talk and laughter of family, with children whizzing in and out, that is something to treasure. I have been fortunate in more ways than I can count, but the thing that makes me luckiest is having a big, warm, loving family.

Our Bloomingdale cookbook expands year by year, as new dishes are added. I think it is a wonderful legacy to pass on to future generations.

SOUPS

Iced Fresh Pea Soup
Cold Cucumber Soup
Fresh Mushroom Soup
Tortilla Soup

PEA SOUP:

3 leeks

1 onion

1 small bunch celery

¼ pound (1 stick) butter

1 tablespoon curry powder

1½ tablespoons flour

4 cans (10½ ounces each)
   concentrated chicken broth

grated zest of 1 orange

2 shallots, finely chopped

½ teaspoon dried marjoram

2 packages (10 ounces each)
   frozen peas, cooked until just
   tender

2 cups half-and-half

avocado balls

CUCUMBER SOUP:

4 cucumbers

2 cups buttermilk, divided

1 quart sour cream

¾ cup lemon juice

2 teaspoons salt

3 tablespoons dill weed

½ cup chopped fresh parsley

8 scallions

MUSHROOM SOUP:

1 pound fresh mushrooms

3 shallots, chopped

5 tablespoons butter

¼ cup flour

3 cups canned beef bouillon, or
   stock

½ teaspoon dried tarragon

1½ cups cream

Iced Fresh Pea Soup

Chop leeks, onion, and celery and brown lightly in butter in a skillet. Stir in the curry powder and flour. Remove to a large saucepan and add the chicken broth. Cook for 30 minutes, then strain and cool.

When soup is cool, add grated zest from orange, shallots, and marjoram, and blend in an electric blender with the cooled peas. Refrigerate. When soup is cold, stir in the half-and-half.

Just before serving, add 3 or 4 small avocado balls (made with melon baller) to float on top of each cup. Serves 6.

Cold Cucumber Soup

Cut 12 thin slices from the unpeeled cucumbers and reserve. Peel, seed, and chop the remaining cucumber. Place half the chopped cucumbers and 1 cup of buttermilk in an electric blender and blend until smooth. Pour into a large bowl. Then place the other half of the chopped cucumbers and 1 cup of buttermilk into the blender. Add sour cream, lemon juice, salt, and dill weed, and blend until smooth. Then add parsley and scallions and blend again until smooth. Decorate the top with cucumber slices. Serves 4 to 6.

Fresh Mushroom Soup

Wash and finely chop mushrooms.

Cook shallots in butter until wilted, then add the mushrooms and simmer for 10 minutes, stirring occasionally. Stir in flour, then add beef bouillon and tarragon. Simmer for 15 minutes, then add cream. Serves 6.

Tortilla Soup

Sauté the onion, jalapeño, oil, garlic, and stew meat, if used, in a large kettle. Add the remaining ingredients, except tortillas and cheese, and simmer for 50 minutes. Add tortillas and cook for 10 minutes. Pour into mugs and sprinkle with cheese. This is very hot, but good. Serves 6 to 8.

Note: When preparing fresh chilies, wear rubber gloves for protection against oils that later can cause a burning sensation on skin.

SALADS

Radicchio and Arugula

Celery Root

Endive and Watercress

Avocado Salad with Warm Vinaigrette

Gingery Cauliflower Salad

Radicchio and Arugula Salad with Roquefort French Dressing

Combine vinegar, salt and pepper to taste. Add oil and cream and beat thoroughly. Stir in Roquefort and lemon juice. Makes about 1 cup dressing. Pour over radicchio and arugula.

Celery Root Salad

Cut celery root into matchstick pieces and toss with salt and lemon juice. Let stand for 30 minutes, then rinse in cold water. Dry with a towel.

Mix mayonnaise with mustard, a sprinkle of lemon juice, and salt and pepper to taste. Combine with celery and marinate 2 to 3 hours or overnight. Serve garnished with parsley. Serves 4.

TORTILLA SOUP:

1 medium onion, chopped

1 jalapeño pepper, chopped

2 tablespoons vegetable oil

2 cloves garlic, minced

2 pounds stew meat (optional)

1 can (14$\frac{1}{2}$ ounces) tomatoes

1 can (5 ounces) Ro-tel tomatoes with chilies

1 can (10$\frac{1}{2}$ ounces) beef broth

1 can (10$\frac{1}{2}$ ounces) chicken broth

1 can (10$\frac{1}{2}$ ounces) tomato soup

1$\frac{1}{2}$ soup cans (15$\frac{3}{4}$ ounces) water

1 teaspoon ground cumin

1 teaspoon chili powder

1 teaspoon salt

$\frac{1}{2}$ teaspoon lemon pepper seasoning

2 teaspoons Worcestershire sauce

3 tablespoons Tabasco

4 tortillas, cut into 1-inch squares

$\frac{1}{4}$ cup grated cheddar cheese

RADICCHIO AND ARUGULA:

$\frac{1}{4}$ cup wine vinegar

$\frac{1}{4}$ teaspoon salt

pepper

$\frac{1}{2}$ cup olive oil

2 tablespoons heavy cream

$\frac{1}{4}$ cup crumbled Roquefort cheese

a few drops of lemon juice

radicchio and arugula

CELERY ROOT:

celery root (celeriac)

1$\frac{1}{2}$ teaspoons salt

2 tablespoons lemon juice

1 cup mayonnaise

4 tablespoons Dijon mustard

sprinkle of lemon juice

salt and pepper

ENDIVE AND WATERCRESS:

4 or 5 firm endive

1 bunch watercress

WATERCRESS DRESSING:

1/2 cup olive oil

3 tablespoons pear vinegar

1/2 cup minced watercress

2 fat shallots, minced

salt and pepper to taste

Endive and Watercress Salad

Clean endive and cut them into thin slices lengthwise. In salad bowl, place the leaves of a large bunch of watercress. Toss lightly with watercress dressing.

WATERCRESS DRESSING:

Place all ingredients in a blender and mix well.

AVOCADO:

2 large tomatoes, peeled, seeded, and diced

1/2 cup chopped basil leaves

4 tablespoons red wine vinegar

1/2 cup olive oil

2 tablespoons Dijon mustard

salt and pepper

2 avocados, halved and pitted

bay leaf for garnish

Avocado Salad with Warm Vinaigrette

In a saucepan, combine tomatoes, basil, vinegar, oil, mustard, and salt and pepper to taste. Bring the mixture to a simmer. Spoon the warm dressing over the avocados and garnish each with a bay leaf. Serves 4.

GINGERY CAULIFLOWER:

1 large cauliflower, trimmed and cut into florets

fresh ginger, 1-inch piece, peeled and julienned

1 carrot, julienned

2 tablespoons white vinegar

1/2 teaspoon sugar

1/4 teaspoon salt

1/8 teaspoon cayenne pepper

1 tablespoon vegetable oil

1/2 teaspoon sesame oil

1 scallion, trimmed, julienne green part and soak in water, slice the white part diagonally into thin ovals

Gingery Cauliflower Salad

Mound the cauliflower florets on a heat-proof plate to resemble a whole head of cauliflower. Scatter the ginger and carrot over the cauliflower.

Combine the vinegar, sugar, salt, and cayenne pepper in a small bowl. Whisk in the vegetable oil and pour the dressing over the cauliflower.

Pour enough water into a large steamer to fill it about 1 inch deep. Put in the heat-proof plate with the cauliflower and cover the steamer, bring to a boil and steam until al dente, about 15 minutes. Let stand until it reaches room temperature.

Drizzle the sesame oil over the cauliflower and scatter the green and white scallion parts on top.

Serve the salad at room temperature or chilled. Serves 6.

FIRST AND MAIN COURSES

Cheese Charlotte
Erlinda's Pork Casserole
Molded Pasta with Prosciutto
Glenn's Quail
Ginger Scallops
Viennese Fried Chicken
Boiled Beef Dinner
Mother's Shepherd's Pie
Chicken Mousse

Cheese Charlotte

Butter each slice of bread, remove the crust, and cut into very small cubes. Sauté green onions in butter until transparent but not brown. Butter a 2-quart casserole dish and arrange a layer of bread cubes on the bottom, placing a generous amount of grated cheese over it. Add a second layer of bread cubes and place remaining cheese over it. Mix the salt, pepper, and mustard together and blend into the milk. Add the minced onions, Tabasco, and the lightly beaten eggs, and mix well. Pour over the bread and cheese mixture. Cover with waxed paper and refrigerate for several hours or overnight.

Remove from the refrigerator and let stand for 1 hour. Then place in a pan of water and bake at 350 degrees for 1 hour or until it is well browned and firm. Serves 6.

9 medium-thick slices white bread
butter
1 bunch finely minced green onions
1½ pounds sharp cheddar cheese (6 cups grated)
1½ teaspoons salt
pepper
½ teaspoon dry mustard
3 cups milk
dash of Tabasco
6 eggs, lightly beaten

৯৯

Many of my most popular dishes are the creation of my wonderful cook, Erlinda. The following pork casserole is unlike any I've ever tasted.

1½ pounds pork tenderloin, trimmed of fat and cut into bite-size pieces

salt and pepper

3 tablespoons flour

5 tablespoons butter, divided

2 tablespoons vegetable oil

2 large onions, halved and sliced

1½ cups chicken stock

1½ cups beer

1 teaspoon arrowroot

2 tablespoons red wine vinegar

3 heaping tablespoons chopped parsley

1 bay leaf

2 teaspoons dried thyme

1 tablespoon olive oil

10 slices French bread, cut ½-inch thick

2 tablespoons Dijon mustard

6 ounces cheddar cheese, grated (1½ cups)

Erlinda's Pork Casserole

Preheat oven to 350 degrees.

Grease a 1½- to 2-quart casserole.

Season the pork with salt and pepper. Dredge with the flour. Heat 2 tablespoons of butter with the vegetable oil in a large saucepan. Over medium heat, cook the onions, stirring occasionally, until they are lightly browned. Transfer the onions to the casserole.

Add the pork to the pan, using a little more oil if needed. Fry until it is golden or light brown on all sides. Add the chicken stock, beer, and arrowroot, and bring the mixture to simmer. Add the vinegar, salt and pepper to taste, and simmer for 2 to 3 minutes.

Remove the pork and arrange it over the onions in the casserole. Pour in the stock mixture, which is slightly thickened. Add 1 heaping tablespoon of parsley, bay leaf, and thyme. Cover the casserole and cook for 1½ to 2 hours or until the pork is tender.

Meanwhile, prepare the topping: heat 1 tablespoon of butter and the olive oil. Toast the bread until lightly brown, on one side only. Set aside and drain. Mix 2 tablespoons of softened butter with mustard and 1 heaping tablespoon parsley. Spread the mixture over the untoasted sides of the bread. Arrange the bread on top of the pork, toasted side down. Sprinkle with cheese. Bake uncovered until the topping is golden, about 30 to 40 minutes. Before serving, remove the bay leaf and sprinkle with 1 heaping tablespoon parsley. Serves 6.

10 slices thin prosciutto

5 cups egg noodles, uncooked

2 cups heavy cream, divided

salt and pepper

½ cup chopped truffles

CREAM-CHIVE SAUCE:

2 cups heavy cream

1 teaspoon arrowroot

salt and white pepper

dash of cayenne pepper

2 tablespoons chives, divided

Molded Pasta with Prosciutto

Grease the bottom and sides of a 11 x 4½ x 3-inch loaf pan. Line lengthwise with greased wax paper for easy un-molding. Line the bottom and sides with prosciutto.

Cook pasta according to package directions. Meanwhile, heat 1½ cups of cream in a saucepan. Season with salt and pepper to taste. Drain the pasta and pour it into the cream. Add the truffles and mix well.

Pour the pasta mixture into the prepared pan. Top it with the remaining ½ cup of cream. Cover the pan with greased wax paper and press lightly over the top with fingers to even out the mixture.

Place it in a bain-marie (water bath). Bake for 1 hour in a 400 degree oven. Remove wax paper and unmold. Serve with Cream-Chive Sauce. Serves 6.

CREAM-CHIVE SAUCE:

In a small, heavy saucepan, heat whipping cream with the arrowroot. Beat until slightly thickened. Season with salt and pepper to taste. Sprinkle with cayenne pepper. Add 1 tablespoon of chives. Mix well. Before serving, sprinkle with remaining chives.

Glenn Bernbaum owns Mortimer's, one of my favorite restaurants in New York. He gave me this recipe to add to my family cookbook.

Glenn's Quail

Split or butterfly the birds and rub each one with a mixture of salt, fresh ground pepper, and thyme. Dribble ¹/₂ cup of cognac over quail and rub it in.

Put vegetable oil and clarified butter in a skillet and heat to hot but not smoking. Sauté quail until brown on all sides. Drain oil from the pan and flambé with ¹/₄ cup of cognac.

Remove birds to heated platter.

Add chicken stock to pan drippings. Add salt and flour to make into gravy. Pour gravy over the quail. Serves 4.

QUAIL:

8 quail

salt and freshly ground pepper

1 pinch thyme

³/₄ cup cognac or brandy, divided

¹/₂ cup vegetable oil

4 tablespoons clarified butter

Ginger Scallops

Cut the carrots into 1¹/₂-inch lengths, ¹/₄-inch thick. Then cut each slice into very thin matchlike strips.

Cut the zucchini into very thin matchlike strips the same size as the carrots. Shred the leek.

Heat 2 tablespoons of the butter in a skillet and add the shallots. Cook briefly, stirring, then add the carrots. Continue cooking and stirring for about 30 seconds, then add the ginger. Cook briefly, stirring, then add the wine. Let the wine reduce

CONTINUED

GINGER SCALLOPS:

1 large carrot, trimmed and
    scraped

1 small zucchini, ends trimmed

1 small leek, trimmed

10 tablespoons butter, divided

2 tablespoons finely chopped
    shallots

2 tablespoons finely chopped
    fresh ginger

¹/₂ cup dry white wine

¹/₂ cup heavy cream

salt and pepper

1¹/₄ pounds bay scallops

almost completely and add the cream, and salt and pepper to taste. Cook over high heat until the sauce is reduced by half.

Add the scallops, zucchini, and leeks. Cook, stirring, about 1 minute and swirl in the remaining 8 tablespoons of butter. Serves 4.

Viennese Fried Chicken

FRIED CHICKEN:

3 broiler chickens, about 2 pounds each, cut into quarters

3 cups flour, sifted with 1 teaspoon salt

4 eggs, lightly beaten with 1 tablespoon water

3 cups fresh bread crumbs, very fine (put in food processor)

vegetable oil and butter, for frying

1/2 cup sizzling melted butter

Dip the chicken pieces in flour until they are well coated, then in the egg and water mixture, and then in the bread crumbs. In a large skillet, heat mixture of oil and butter to a depth of 2 inches, and fry 25 to 30 minutes, turning pieces to cook all sides. Transfer to a roasting pan and drizzle butter over the chicken. After all the chicken is fried, put roasting pan in the oven at 350 degrees for 10 minutes. Serves 6.

Boiled Beef Dinner

BOILED BEEF:

1 beef brisket (3 to 3 1/2 pounds)

6 medium carrots

2 large onions, cut in half

2 stalks celery, chopped

1 tablespoon salt

1/4 teaspoon pepper

1 tablespoon whole pickling spice

water

6 to 8 small potatoes

Place meat in a large pot. Add whole carrots, halved onions, chopped celery, salt and pepper, pickling spice, and water to cover meat and vegetables. Cover and simmer for 3 to 4 hours. Do not boil. About 30 minutes before beef is done, peel strip around center of potatoes and add them to the stew. Remove meat to platter and arrange vegetables around it. Serve with horseradish or horseradish sauce. Serves 8 to 12.

HORSERADISH SAUCE:

Blend 1 cup sour cream with 1/4 cup horseradish. Add Tabasco and salt to taste.

ஒ

My mother served this simple dish as long ago as I can remember. It is a surprisingly easy way to use leftover lamb and it remains a favorite in the family cookbook.

Mother's Shepherd's Pie

Grind meat with raw carrots and onions, which have been chopped separately. Place in casserole and add flour, salt and pepper, a couple of shakes of ketchup, and bouillon. Cook 1 hour in a 350-degree oven. Cover with mashed potatoes and brown. Serves 6.

Chicken Mousse

Purée chicken in a food processor. Add eggs one at a time until smooth. Add salt, white pepper, and Tabasco. Slowly add heavy cream until smooth. Transfer to a bowl: Sauté shallots and red pepper in butter until tender. Stir in chicken mixture along with pistachios.

Place a 16-inch piece of plastic wrap on counter and spoon mixture down the center. Shape mixture into a 12-inch long roll and wrap tightly in plastic wrap, twisting ends to seal. Place roll on 16-inch length of foil, seal, and twist ends. Place roll in roasting pan large enough to hold easily, cover with simmering water, and cook 45 minutes, or until roll is cooked through. Remove from water, drain, chill, and cut into slices. Serve with Avocado and Red Pepper sauces (recipes on page 176). Serves 8.

SHEPHERD'S PIE:
1 leg of lamb (leftover pieces)
1/2 cup carrots, diced
1/2 cup onions, diced
3 to 4 tablespoons flour
salt and pepper
2 shakes of ketchup
1 can (10 1/2 ounces) beef bouillon
mashed potatoes to cover

CHICKEN MOUSSE:
4 boneless chicken breasts, skinned and cubed
2 eggs
1/2 teaspoon salt
dash of white pepper
dash of Tabasco
1/2 cup heavy cream
1 tablespoon minced shallots
2 tablespoons minced sweet red (bell) pepper
1 tablespoon butter or margarine
1/2 cup chopped pistachios

SIDE DISHES

Emma's Artichokes
Asparagus Polonaise
Kacey's Tomato Pie
Potatoes Dauphinoise

❧

My family cookbook includes very few vegetable dishes, for one reason. I prefer to serve my vegetables plain and simple, and if possible, straight from the garden. I grow tomatoes, zucchini, squash, corn, string beans, snap peas, and carrots, and they're best fresh, blanched or steamed, and tossed with a little butter. Vegetables covered with sauces not only lose their health benefits, but their taste as well.

ટે♪

Emma is a woman who used to cook for me. She prepared artichokes in this simple way.

Emma's Artichokes

ARTICHOKES:
4 artichokes
2 lemons
water
peppercorns
cracked pepper
salt

Trim artichokes and place in a large pot. Squeeze in lemon juice and add the lemon rinds. Cover with cold water and add the seasonings to taste.

Bring to a boil, then reduce heat to simmer. Simmer for 45 minutes to 1 hour. Test a leaf to see if it's tender. When ready, pour off the water, leaving about 1 inch in the pan. Turn the artichokes upside down to drain. Serves 4.

Asparagus Polonaise

ASPARAGUS:
12 tablespoons (1$\frac{1}{2}$ sticks) butter
3 hard-cooked eggs
3 tablespoons lemon juice
salt and pepper
4 pounds asparagus, cooked

Melt butter. Add to hard-cooked eggs, sieved, tablespoons of lemon juice, and salt and pepper to taste. Pour over asparagus. Serves 8 to 10.

Kacey's Tomato Pie

TOMATO PIE:
9-inch pie crust, homemade or
    commercial
tomatoes
salt and pepper
sweet fresh basil, chopped
chopped fresh chives
1 cup mayonnaise
1 cup grated sharp cheddar
    cheese

Kacey McCoy is a charming friend of my daughter-in-law Justine. She loves to cook, and has contributed many recipes to my family cookbook. This Tomato Pie is a perfect accompaniment to beef or lamb, or can be served by itself with a salad.

Preheat oven to 400 degrees.

Prebake the pie crust for 10 minutes to avoid sogginess.

Peel, seed, and thickly slice enough ripe tomatoes to fill and mound slightly in the pie crust. Sprinkle with salt and freshly ground black pepper, chopped basil, and chopped chives to suit your taste. Combine the cheese and mayonnaise and spread it over the tomatoes. (If you like, you can mix half fat-free and half regular mayonnaise to make a lighter dish.)

Bake until brown–approximately 35 minutes. Serves 6 to 8.

*H*ere is one of my daughter-in-law Justine's specialties.

Potatoes Dauphinoise

Preheat oven to 400 degrees.

Rub garlic around the bottom and sides of a rectangular glass baking dish. Combine milk and crème fraîche and let stand. (You can make your own crème fraîche by combining 1 cup of whole milk with 1 cup of sour cream. Cover with plastic wrap, and leave at room temperature until it thickens, up to 24 hours, then refrigerate.) Wash, peel, and thinly slice potatoes and lay them on paper towels to absorb excess liquid.

Place 1 layer of potato slices on the bottom of the dish in rows, then dot with butter, salt and pepper, and a sprinkle of cheese. Make 3 or 4 layers. After the final layer, pour milk mixture over the entire dish and bake for 1 1/2 to 2 hours or until the mixture is bubbly and brown. Serves 10 to 12.

12 White Rose potatoes
equal amounts whole milk and
    crème fraîche
1 to 2 cups grated Swiss cheese
garlic
butter
salt and pepper

SAUCES AND DRESSINGS

Gorgonzola Dressing
Lorenzo Dressing
Sweet and Tangy Mustard
Avocado Sauce
Red Pepper Sauce
Lisa's Tomato Sauce for Pasta
Ann's Version of Mother's Mint Sauce
Le Notre Dessert Syrup

Gorgonzola Dressing

Combine in a mixing bowl red wine vinegar, olive oil, salt and pepper to taste, and Gorgonzola. The mixture should be lumpy. Serve over sliced tomatoes alternating with slices of red onion. Makes 1/2 cup dressing.

1 tablespoon red wine vinegar
3 tablespoons olive oil
salt and pepper
1/4 pound Gorgonzola

LORENZO DRESSING:
2/3 cup olive oil
1/3 cup vinegar
1 teaspoon salt
dash of paprika
1 cup chili sauce
1 cup chopped watercress

MUSTARD SAUCE:
2/3 cup dry mustard
1 cup sugar
3 large eggs
2/3 cup white wine vinegar

AVOCADO SAUCE:
3 small or 1 large avocado
1/4 cup cilantro leaves
1/4 cup mayonnaise
2 tablespoons lime juice
dash Tabasco
dash salt
dash white pepper

RED PEPPER SAUCE:
2 sweet red peppers
2 teaspoons balsamic vinegar
1 teaspoon sugar
1/8 teaspoon minced garlic
dash salt
dash white pepper

This is a dressing I often use with cole slaw.

Lorenzo Dressing

Stir all ingredients together thoroughly. Serve cold. Makes about 2 1/2 cups.

This sauce is wonderful with baked ham.

Sweet and Tangy Mustard

Combine the dry mustard and sugar in the top of a glass double boiler. Beat with a whisk until smooth. Beat in the eggs and vinegar.

Place over boiling water and beat constantly for 5 to 7 minutes until the mixture has thickened and appears slightly foamy. Pour into another container to stop the cooking. Makes about 2 cups.

I like to serve this, along with the Red Pepper Sauce that follows, with cold Chicken Mousse (recipe on page 173). It makes an interesting combination of flavors and colors.

Avocado Sauce

Peel and pit avocado. Purée with cilantro, mayonnaise, lime juice, Tabasco, salt, and white pepper. If sauce is too thick, add water to thin. Makes about 1 cup.

Red Pepper Sauce

Place peppers on the rack of a broiler pan. Broil about 5 inches from heating unit, turning until charred on all sides. Remove, place at once in paper bag, and close tightly. Let stand for 10 minutes. Peel and seed peppers. Purée in a food processor or blender with vinegar, sugar, garlic, salt, and pepper. Chill. Makes about 3/4 cup.

❧

My daughter Lisa is a natural cook who can throw ingredients together without using precise measurements and have the end result turn out right. She has a special talent for sauces, which are always rich and flavorful. This spaghetti sauce is the best.

Lisa's Tomato Sauce for Pasta

In a large skillet, heat oil, and add onion and garlic until lightly golden. Add diced bacon and sauté until crisp. Add tomatoes, salt, pepper to taste, and basil, and stir well with a wooden spoon. Let simmer for 20 minutes, stirring. Makes 3 to 4 cups.

6 tablespoons olive oil
1 medium yellow onion, chopped
1 garlic clove
2 tablespoons bacon, diced
1 can (35 ounces) Italian plum
    tomatoes, hand crushed
$1/2$ teaspoon salt
pepper
6 to 8 large fresh basil leaves,
    minced

❧

Ann is a German lady who has been with my family forever. She worked for my mother for many years, and today she still works for me. Here is her variation of my mother's special mint sauce, which is served with lamb dishes.

Ann's Version of Mother's Mint Sauce

Bring lemon juice and water to a boil. Add sugar.
Cool. When cold, quickly chop and add mint leaves. Mint turns brown if chopped too soon. Makes about $1^1/2$ cups.

$3/4$ cup lemon juice
$1/4$ cup water
1 cup sugar
1 cup mint leaves

Le Notre Dessert Syrup

Bring water and sugar to a boil. Remove from heat and cool. Then add Kirsch or Grand Marnier. Serve lukewarm or chilled.

$2/3$ cup water
$1/2$ cup sugar
3 tablespoons Kirsch or Grand
    Marnier

Note: Liquor may be replaced with a mixture of 3 tablespoons of water and $3/4$ teaspoon of vanilla, if desired. Serve over fresh fruit. Makes about 1 cup.

DESSERTS AND SWEETS

❧

*A*s you can see, we are big dessert lovers in this family! Like most people today, we are always watching our weight and nutrition. But I think if you're careful, you can do that without sacrificing the simple pleasures of a homemade cake or ice cream. Small portions are the secret. With my eight grand-children dropping by, homemade cookies are a must.

Pecan Fingers

1/2 pound (2 sticks) butter
1/2 cup confectioners' sugar
2 cups sifted flour
1/8 teaspoon salt
1 cup chopped pecans
2 teaspoons vanilla

Preheat oven to 325 degrees.

Cream butter and mix in sugar. Add flour, salt, pecans, and vanilla. Form into small fingers on a well-greased cookie sheet. Bake for 15 minutes. Makes 3 to 4 dozen.

Best Brownies Ever

Preheat oven to 350 degrees.

Line the bottom of a 9-inch square pan with greased parchment paper or aluminum foil. Resift flour with baking powder and salt. Melt butter with chocolate in a double boiler or heavy saucepan over very low heat. Cool.

Beat eggs with sugar until light in color. Stir in chocolate mixture and 4 tablespoons of amaretto. Add flour mixture and blend. Stir in nuts.

Turn into prepared pan. Bake for 30 to 35 minutes or until the top springs back when touched lightly in the center and the edges begin to pull away from the pan. Remove from the oven and cool completely. Do not overcook. Brush top with remaining 2 tablespoons of amaretto. Yield: 2 dozen.

1$\frac{1}{2}$ cups sifted flour
$\frac{1}{2}$ teaspoon baking powder
$\frac{1}{2}$ teaspoon salt
12 tablespoons (1$\frac{1}{2}$ sticks) butter or margarine
3 ounces unsweetened chocolate
3 eggs
2 cups sugar
6 tablespoons amaretto, divided
1 to 1$\frac{1}{2}$ cup chopped almonds or walnuts

Isabellas

Preheat oven to 350 degrees.

Cream butter and sugar until light in color. Mix in vanilla, then flour, oats, and salt. Chill thoroughly. Shape into small balls and place 3 inches apart on ungreased baking sheet. Flatten balls with a fork. Bake for 12 to 15 minutes. Sprinkle with confectioners' sugar. Yield: 2 dozen.

$\frac{1}{2}$ pound (2 sticks) butter
$\frac{1}{2}$ cup sugar
1 teaspoon vanilla
1$\frac{1}{4}$ cups flour
1$\frac{1}{2}$ cups rolled oats
dash of salt
confectioners' sugar

Most Popular Cookies

Preheat oven to 325 degrees.

Cream together butter and sugars until mixture is light and fluffy. Add egg, mixing well, then vegetable oil, mixing well. Add oats, cornflakes, coconut, and walnuts, stirring well. Then add flour, baking soda, salt, and vanilla. Mix well and form into balls the size of small walnuts. Place on ungreased cookie sheet and flatten with a fork dipped in water. Bake for 12 minutes. Yield: 8 dozen.

$\frac{1}{2}$ pound (2 sticks) butter
1 cup granulated sugar
1 cup brown sugar, firmly packed
1 egg
1 cup vegetable oil
1 cup rolled oats
1 cup crushed cornflakes
$\frac{1}{2}$ cup shredded coconut
$\frac{1}{2}$ cup chopped walnuts
3$\frac{1}{2}$ cups sifted flour
1 teaspoon baking soda
1 teaspoon salt
1 teaspoon vanilla

ઃ

My Texas friend Ed gave me this recipe. The children love it.

Ed's Potato Chip Cookies

POTATO CHIP COOKIES:
1 pound (4 sticks) butter
1¼ cups sugar
1 teaspoon vanilla
1½ cups crushed potato chips
3 cups sifted flour

Preheat oven to 350 degrees.

Cream butter with sugar, and add vanilla. Crush potato chips by rolling them between waxed paper sheets. Add to flour, then add dry mixture to creamed mixture. Mix well. Drop by small teaspoonfuls on ungreased cookie sheet. Bake for 12 minutes.

Irish Lace Cookies

IRISH LACE COOKIES:
¾ cup brown sugar, packed
¼ pound (1 stick) butter
2 tablespoons flour
2 tablespoons milk
1 teaspoon vanilla extract
1¼ cups oatmeal

Preheat oven to 350 degrees.

Cream together sugar and butter, then beat in the flour, milk, and vanilla. Stir in the oatmeal and mix well.

Drop the mixture by the spoonful onto an ungreased cookie sheet. Bake 10 to 15 minutes. Yield: 2 dozen.

Peanut Butter-Chocolate Chip Cookies

PEANUT BUTTER COOKIES:
½ pound (2 sticks) unsalted
    butter, room temperature
1 cup firmly packed dark brown
    sugar
½ cup granulated sugar
1½ cups chunky peanut butter
1 egg
2 teaspoons vanilla
pinch of salt
1½ cups unbleached all-purpose
    flour
2 cups (12 ounces) semisweet
    chocolate chips
1 cup glazed peanuts

Preheat oven to 350 degrees.

Grease cookie sheet.

Cream butter until light; gradually beat in sugars and continue beating until fluffy. Add the peanut butter and blend until it's fluffy. Add egg, vanilla, and salt and beat again until mixture is fluffy.

Using a rubber spatula, quickly fold in flour, chocolate chips, and peanuts. Dough will be stiff. Drop by tablespoon on greased cookie sheet, then flatten to 4 inches round. Space cookies 1 inch apart. Bake until golden brown, about 17 minutes. Yield: 3 to 4 dozen.

Chocolate Angel Food Cake

Preheat oven to 375 degrees.

Sift the cake flour, cocoa, and confectioners' sugar together 3 times into a medium-size mixing bowl.

Mix the egg whites, cream of tartar, salt, and vanilla and almond extracts. Beat at a high speed until the whites do not slide when you tip the bowl. Add the fine sugar gradually as you continue beating. Stop beating when all the sugar is mixed in. You should have a meringue consistency.

Transfer the meringue to a very large mixing bowl. Sift about a quarter of the flour mixture over the whites and fold it in carefully. Sift and fold in the rest, about one-third at a time.

Pour the batter into an ungreased tube pan, and cut straight down through the batter with a knife several times to release any bubbles.

Bake the cake for 30 to 35 minutes or until it is firm to the touch. Turn the pan upside down onto the neck of a bottle for at least an hour until it is thoroughly cooled. Remove from the pan by running a knife around the edges to loosen it. Frost with Cocoa-Rum Icing.

COCOA RUM ICING:

Mix the cocoa and confectioners' sugar together in a small mixing bowl. In a separate bowl, beat the butter or margarine until creamy. Beat in half the cocoa-sugar mixture, then add the vanilla, rum, and half the evaporated milk and beat thoroughly. Add the remaining cocoa-sugar mixture and beat well. Add the remaining evaporated milk and beat for several minutes until the icing reaches the desired spreading consistency.

ANGEL FOOD CAKE:

$^3/_4$ cup sifted cake flour

$^1/_3$ cup unsweetened cocoa

$1^1/_2$ cups sifted confectioners' sugar

13 egg whites, room temperature

$1^1/_2$ teaspoons cream of tartar

$^1/_4$ teaspoon salt

$1^1/_2$ teaspoons vanilla

scant $^1/_2$ teaspoon almond extract

1 cup extra-fine granulated sugar

ICING:

$^3/_4$ cup unsweetened cocoa

4 cups confectioners' sugar

$^1/_4$ pound (1 stick) butter or margarine

$1^1/_2$ teaspoons vanilla

5 teaspoons dark rum

$^1/_2$ cup evaporated milk

Erlinda's Sponge Cake

Preheat oven to 300 degrees.

Cook sugar and water to make a syrup. Beat egg yolks until they're a light color, then add the sugar mixture little by little.

Fold in flour and salt (sifted 3 times). Beat egg whites with cream of tartar and fold them in.

Bake in a tube pan for $1^1/_2$ hours. Invert pan onto a funnel or bottle to cool.

SPONGE CAKE:

$1^1/_2$ cups sugar

$^1/_2$ cup water

8 eggs, separated

1 cup flour

1 teaspoon salt

1 teaspoon cream of tartar

181

Rum Cake

RUM CAKE:

2 eggs

1 1/2 cups sugar, divided

3 tablespoons cold water

1 cup sifted cake flour

1 1/2 teaspoons baking powder

1/2 teaspoon salt

1 tablespoon vanilla

1/4 cup water

juice of 1 lemon

1/2 cup dark Jamaican rum

RUM CREAM:

1 envelope (1/4 ounce) unflavored
   gelatin

1/2 cup cold water

4 egg yolks

1/2 cup sugar

2 cups milk

4 tablespoons dark Jamaican rum

1 cup heavy cream, whipped

slivered almonds for garnish

Although there are three steps involved here, it is wise to start them all at the same time for the baking, cooling, and thickening process takes time.

Preheat oven to 350 degrees.

Beat eggs in a mixer until very thick and light.

Add 1 cup sugar gradually, beating it in. Add water and blend with a folding motion. Resift flour with baking powder and salt, and fold into the first mixture. Add vanilla.

Pour batter into a 10-inch springform pan and bake for about 30 minutes or until the center is firm. Cool cake in the pan.

Mix remaining 1/2 cup of sugar with 1/4 cup of water and the juice of 1 lemon. Boil the mixture for 10 minutes. Cool and add 1/2 cup of dark Jamaican rum.

Baste the cooled cake with the rum mixture, about 2 tablespoons at a time. When that has been absorbed, add 2 tablespoons more and continue until the entire mixture has been used. Leave cake in pan and spread with Rum Cream.

RUM CREAM:

Soften gelatin in cold water. Put egg yolks in top of double boiler (an enameled one is best), beat slightly with fork, add sugar, add milk, and place over hot water. Cook, stirring constantly, until thickened to consistency of custard. Be careful it doesn't curdle. Remove from the hot water, pour some of the custard into the gelatin, then add the rest of the custard. Cool, but do not allow it to set, then add rum. Put into refrigerator until thick but not too firm (or put into freezer for one-half hour). Fold custard carefully into whipped cream. Spread on cake and chill until serving time.

At serving time, remove side of pan, but not the bottom. Sprinkle with slivered almonds. Serves 10 to 12.

Lady Baltimore Cake

Preheat oven to 350 degrees.

Cream butter until it's soft, then gradually beat in 1½ cups of sugar until the mixture is light and fluffy. Beat in vanilla.

Resift flour with baking powder and salt. Add this to creamed mixture alternately with milk.

Beat the egg whites until they form soft peaks. Then gradually beat in the remaining ½ cup of sugar until stiff but not dry. Fold into the batter. Spoon the batter into 3 greased and floured 8-inch layer cake pans. Bake for 25 minutes or until the cake is done. Remove and let stand for several minutes before turning onto wire racks to cool. Stack layers with frosting in between and decorate with walnut halves.

FROSTING:

Combine raisins and dates with orange juice or brandy. Add walnuts and set aside.

Combine sugar, water, and salt in a deep saucepan. Cover and bring to a boil. Remove the cover and boil rapidly to 248 degrees on a candy thermometer.

Beat egg whites until they form soft peaks. Pour syrup in a thin, steady stream onto the egg whites. Continue beating until the mixture begins to hold its shape. Beat in the vanilla and lemon extract.

Add fruit mixture to one third of the frosting and leave the remainder plain. The fruited portion is for between layers, and the plain is for the top and sides of the cake.

Coconut Pudding with Caramel Sauce

Let cream come to a boil. Add the gelatin, which has been soaked in a little cold water, and the sugar. When ingredients have dissolved, cool, and add flavoring and coconut. Fold in the whipped cream.

Pour into a mold and chill until firm. When ready, remove from the mold and sprinkle with the fresh coconut. Serve with caramel sauce.

CARAMEL SAUCE:

Combine butter and sugar, then add egg yolks, cream and salt. Cook in a double boiler until smooth and creamy. Cool and add vanilla.

LADY BALTIMORE CAKE:

½ pound (2 sticks) butter or margarine

2 cups sugar, divided

1 teaspoon vanilla

3 cups sifted cake flour

1 tablespoon baking powder

1 teaspoon salt

1 cup milk

6 egg whites

walnut halves

FROSTING:

⅓ cup raisins

⅓ cup dates

2 tablespoons orange juice or brandy

⅔ cup chopped walnuts

3 cups sugar

1 cup water

⅛ teaspoon salt

3 egg whites

½ teaspoon vanilla

½ teaspoon lemon extract

COCONUT PUDDING:

2 cups half-and-half

2 tablespoons unflavored gelatin

1 cup sugar

1 teaspoon almond extract

2 cups fresh coconut, grated

1½ pints heavy cream, whipped

CARAMEL SAUCE:

1 tablespoon butter

1 pound (2⅓ cups) light brown sugar

2 egg yolks

1 cup heavy cream

⅛ teaspoon salt

1 teaspoon vanilla

Coconut Cake with Coconut Icing

COCONUT CAKE:

2¼ cups sifted cake flour

3 teaspoons baking powder

⅛ teaspoon salt

3 eggs, separated

1½ cups sugar, divided

¾ cup vegetable shortening

¼ cup fresh shredded coconut

¾ cup coconut water (juice)

½ teaspoon almond extract

COCONUT ICING:

1½ cups sugar

¼ cup water

¼ teaspoon cream of tartar

dash of salt

2 egg whites

1 teaspoon almond extract

½ cup fresh shredded coconut

Preheat oven to 375 degrees.

Sift together flour, baking powder, and salt. Beat egg whites until they form soft peaks. Add ½ cup of sugar, 2 tablespoons at a time, and beat the mixture until stiff peaks form. Cream the shortening. Add remaining cup of sugar gradually, creaming until fluffy. Beat egg yolks and blend into creamed mixture. Stir in shredded coconut. Add dry ingredients alternately with coconut water. Stir in almond extract, then fold in egg whites.

Turn into 2 greased and lightly floured 9-inch cake pans. Bake for 25 to 30 minutes or until cake springs back when touched lightly. Cool cakes in pans for 5 to 10 minutes, then turn out onto wire racks to cool completely. Frost with fresh coconut icing.

FRESH COCONUT ICING:

Mix sugar, water, cream of tartar, salt, and egg whites in the top of a double boiler. Place over boiling water and beat with an electric beater until stiff peaks form. Remove from heat and continue to beat until thick enough to spread. Add almond extract and shredded coconut. Frost cake and sprinkle generously with additional shredded coconut.

&

Alfred always loved this. I made it every year for his birthday.

Dobos Torte

1 cup flour

7 eggs, separated

⅛ teaspoon salt

1 cup confectioners' sugar

FILLING:

1 pound bittersweet chocolate

3 tablespoons water

3 eggs

1½ cups confectioners' sugar

scant ½ pound (2 sticks) butter,

1 teaspoon vanilla

Preheat oven to 375 degrees.

Sift flour once, measure, and sift 4 more times. Beat egg yolks, salt, and sugar until thick. Fold in flour and stiffly beaten (but not dry) egg whites. Spread thin layers of dough on buttered and floured layer cake pans. (Removable bottoms are preferred.) Bake for 6 to 8 minutes. Remove at once from pans and repeat the process until all the dough is used. This will make 6 or 7 layers; increase the recipe to make more layers.

FILLING:

Melt chocolate with water in a double boiler. Mix eggs and sugar, add to chocolate and cook until thick, stirring constantly. Remove from stove, cool, add vanilla and butter, which has been creamed until light, and beat until blended.

Spread between layers, and cover top and sides. To keep layers from slipping, put toothpicks through top layers until the filling sets. Allow the torte to set 24 hours before serving.

If you like, you may glaze the top instead of using filling. To make glaze, melt 3 tablespoons of sugar in a skillet. Put it over the top and spread with a hot knife.

෧

*H*omemade ice cream was always a favorite dessert in the Bloomingdale household, and the children have picked it up. We all love to experiment with different flavors. For most of the following recipes, you'll need an ice cream maker. This Praline Ice Cream is my absolute favorite.

Praline Ice Cream

Place the pecans in a buttered 8-inch pie pan.

In a skillet, combine 1 cup of the sugar and $^1/_4$ cup cold water. Cook the mixture over low heat, stirring until the sugar is dissolved. Turn the heat to high and continue cooking until the mixture is caramelized. Pour over the pecans and let cool completely. Break the praline into pieces, then grind in a food processor until it is coarse.

In the top of a double boiler, whisk together the whole eggs, egg yolk, salt, and remaining $^3/_4$ cup of sugar. Whisk the mixture until it is light. Scald the cream and milk together and add it to the mixture in a stream. Cook the custard over boiling water, stirring, until it is thick enough to coat the spoon. Transfer to a bowl and stir in the vanilla. Let the custard cool slightly, covered with waxed paper, then chill it for about 3 hours in the refrigerator.

Freeze the custard in an ice cream freezer. Before it is frozen solid, stir in the praline and continue freezing. Makes about 1 quart.

1 cup pecans, toasted lightly
$1^3/_4$ cups sugar, divided
2 large eggs
1 egg yolk
$^1/_8$ teaspoon salt
$1^1/_2$ cups heavy cream
1 cup milk
1 tablespoon vanilla

PEACHY ICE CREAM:

12 medium peaches, ripened,
    peeled, and pitted (3 pounds)
2³/4 cups sugar
1 tablespoon lemon juice
1¹/2 quarts heavy cream
¹/4 teaspoon salt
1 teaspoon vanilla
1 teaspoon almond extract

CARAMEL ICE CREAM:

1¹/2 cups sugar, divided
1 cup boiling water
4 cups heavy cream
6 egg yolks, lightly beaten
pinch of salt
1 teaspoon vanilla
toasted almonds

CHOCOLATE ICE CREAM:

4 large egg yolks
¹/2 cup milk
³/4 cup unsweetened cocoa
    powder
1 cup sugar
2 cups heavy cream, chilled
2 teaspoons vanilla
¹/8 teaspoon salt

LEMON ICE CREAM:

¹/2 cup lemon juice
zest of one lemon, grated
1 cup sugar
1 cup heavy cream
1 cup half-and-half

Peachy Ice Cream

Force peaches through a sieve or food mill. Stir in the sugar and lemon juice and set aside for 20 minutes.

Blend the cream, salt, and extracts. Mix well with the peaches. Make in an ice cream freezer according to manufacturer's directions. Makes approximately 1¹/2 quarts.

Caramel Ice Cream

Cook 1 cup of sugar in a heavy skillet until it melts and becomes golden. Add 1 cup boiling water and stir until the sugar is dissolved. Then bring to a boil and cook about 10 minutes until it becomes a thick caramel syrup.

Scald 4 cups of heavy cream and mix thoroughly with ¹/2 cup sugar. Pour this very slowly over 6 lightly beaten egg yolks, stirring constantly.

Pour mixture into a saucepan and cook over medium heat, stirring, until it is thickened. Add salt, vanilla, and ³/4 of the caramel syrup. Blend thoroughly, then pour into the ice cream machine and freeze. Serve with remaining caramel sauce and toasted almond slices. Makes about 1 quart.

Rich Chocolate Ice Cream

In a mixing bowl, beat the egg yolks with the milk. Mix the cocoa and sugar, and add to the egg yolk/milk mixture a little at a time, beating well. Set the bowl over a pan of simmering water and heat the mixture for 7 to 10 minutes or until it is thick and double the volume.

Set the bowl in a larger bowl filled with cold water and beat the mixture until it is cold. Then beat in the cream, vanilla, and salt. Make in an ice cream freezer. Makes about 1 quart.

Lisa's Lemon Ice Cream

Beat all ingredients together, and taste for sweetness. Add more sugar if desired. Make in an ice cream freezer. Makes about 1 quart.

Bertie's 3 Fruit Flavor Ice Cream

Mix together mashed bananas, orange juice, lemon juice, and sugar until the sugar is dissolved.

Strain and cool, then add milk and cream and pour into ice cream freezer. Serves 10 to 12.

FRUIT ICE CREAM:
3 or 4 bananas
juice of 3 oranges
juice of 3 lemons
3 cups sugar
3 cups milk
3 cups heavy cream (or half-and-half)

Orange Ice with Orange Sauce

ORANGE SAUCE:

Drain the oranges and measure the liquid. In a saucepan, combine the liquid with an equal amount of sugar and cook, stirring, until the sugar melts. Stir in the orange liqueur and continue to cook for 3 minutes. Pour the mixture over the orange sections and chill overnight.

ORANGE ICE:

Boil water with sugar for 5 minutes. Let cool and add orange juice, lemon juice, and orange zest. Let mixture stand for about 10 minutes, then strain. Make in an ice cream freezer.

Spoon the orange ice into sherbet glasses and top with orange sauce. Serves 6.

ORANGE SAUCE:
2 cans (11 ounces each) mandarin oranges
sugar
$1/3$ cup orange liqueur

ORANGE ICE:
4 cups water
2 cups sugar
2 cups orange juice
$1/4$ cup lemon juice
zest of 2 oranges, finely grated

❧

My daughter-in-law Polly always makes this candy for Christmas, but it's great any time of the year.

Polly's Candy

Boil butter and sugar in a heavy saucepan for 5 minutes. Then add water, 1 tablespoon at a time. Cook to hard crack stage—300 degrees on a candy thermometer, about 20 minutes. Be sure to stir constantly to keep from burning. The mixture starts getting thicker and a dark caramel color.

Pour the candy onto unbuttered cookie sheets. Spread quickly with a spatula to desired thickness (about $1/4$ inch). Break chocolate into sections and place on top of the hot candy mixture. Let set for a few seconds until the chocolate gets soft. Then spread it over candy until smooth. Sprinkle almonds on top. Allow to cool, then break into pieces.

1 pound (4 sticks) butter
1 pound sugar
4 tablespoons water
1 pound milk chocolate (Hershey bars)
2 to 3 cups sliced almonds, lightly toasted

Appendix

** Egg Caution Note: This recipe calls for uncooked eggs. Be sure to use clean, uncracked eggs. Because of the possibility of salmonella, we would not recommend this recipe for persons in a high risk group for contracting food poisoning. This group includes the elderly, the very young, the chronically ill, pregnant women, or others with a weakened immune system.

** Crème Fraîche: You can make your own crème fraîche by combining 1 cup of whole milk with 1 cup of sour cream. Cover with plastic wrap, and leave at room temperature until it thickens, up to 24 hours, then refrigerate.

Index